THE PROGRESSIVE VIRUS

WHY YOU CAN'T PERMIT IT TO GO **FORWARD**

DR. ANTHONY NAPOLEON

"The Progressive Virus: Why You Can't Permit it to Go Forward," by Anthony Napoleon. ISBN 978-1-62137-130-4 (Softcover), 978-1-62137-137-3 (Hardcover), 978-1-62137-138-0 (eBook).

Published 2012 by Virtualbookworm.com Publishing Inc., P.O. Box 9949, College Station, TX 77842, US. ©2012, Anthony Napoleon. All rights reserved. No part of this publication may be reproduced, stored in a retrieval system, or transmitted in any form or by any means, electronic, mechanical, recording or otherwise, without the prior written permission of Anthony Napoleon.

Manufactured in the United States of America.

Table of Contents

CHAPTER ONE

Introduction and History

THIS IS A BOOK ABOUT an epidemic infecting America and much of the Western world. The epidemic I make reference to is not some rogue virus or genetically engineered bacterium. The sickness infecting America involves the widespread adoption of a psychological belief system. This belief system is named progressivism.

Progressivism declares that no objective reality exists but for the perception of man. It assumes that man is born as a tabula rasa and that his environment, which is characterized by social injustice, accounts for why some people do not achieve financial and social wealth. Progressives believe that those who do achieve financial and social wealth have done so by directly or indirectly oppressing the have-nots. Progressivism seeks to restore the inequity between the haves and the have-nots by deemphasizing equal opportunity in favor of government enforced equal outcomes, regardless of merit, talent, effort or inheritance. Citizen's sense of entitlement is

1

fundamental to the progressive's notion of social justice.

Progressivism did not appear overnight but developed incrementally as men changed their notions about life itself. An early iteration of progressivism undoubtedly appeared naturally during the dawn of man, but never fully developed, nor did it spread to infect large portions of the population due to immune system barriers and no efficient way that others could be easily infected en masse.

The immune system barriers that protected early man were comprised of barrier realities, e.g., the need for food, shelter, clothing and the presence of natural competition. These realities consumed the undivided attention of early man. Philosophical notions necessarily took a back seat to fending off predators, scavenging for food and dealing with life and death on a daily basis. It is no coincidence that the idle rich generated the first iteration of the progressive virus.

Rene Descartes was an early developer of the progressive virus who wrote some of its first DNA code in the mid-17th century. Descartes's declaration: "Je pense donc je suis; (I think, therefore I am) became a core building block of progressivism. [1] Descartes wrote:

---

[1] Descarte's declaration was known as the Cogito Ergo Sum argument in the English speaking world.

"I have convinced myself that there is absolutely nothing in the world, no sky, no earth, no minds, no bodies. Does it now follow that I, too, do not exist? No. If I convinced myself of something [or thought anything at all], then I certainly existed. But there is a deceiver of supreme power and cunning who deliberately and constantly deceives me. In that case, I, too, undoubtedly exist, if he deceives me; and let him deceive me as much as he can, he will never bring it about that I am nothing, so long as I think that I am something. So, after considering everything very thoroughly, I must finally conclude that the proposition, I am, I exist, is necessarily true whenever it is put forward by me or conceived in my mind. [2]

Descartes had the time and resources to be fascinated with the proposition that he caused his own existence. His fascination with such matters was not readily contagious because, in part, existent French and English mores functioned as a natural barrier to the fledgling virus he was helping to create. Notably, Englishmen John Locke and Thomas Hobbes had erected barriers to the virus. Locke imbued thinkers of the 17th century with the

---

[2] Descartes. Meditationes de prima philosophia, (Meditations on First Philosophy). éd. de Amstelodami, ex typographia Blavania, 1685, Vicifons. AT VII 25; CSM II 16–17.

anti-progressive notion of inalienable rights. Locke's God given rights included life, liberty and property. Hobbes argued for the notion that man was free (naturally) to engage in behavior not explicitly prohibited by law. [3] The importance of declaring that man was free was remarkable for its time, given the dominance of the British monarchy and the French ruling class.

The 18th Century produced thinkers who constructed fire walls to the fledgling virus in their midst. Important immune system boosters included Charles Montesquieu and Voltaire. These men disrupted the virus's ability to replicate.

Montesquieu espoused the idea that governments should be separated into three branches; the executive, legislative and judicial. His tri-part governmental thesis was designed to serve as a structural limit on what would turn out to be a necessary component of a widespread progressive infection: centralized power.

Voltaire advocated for the preeminence of the individual, not the collective. He asserted that man had a God given right to a free trial and freedom from state mandated religions. Whenever man believes that his rights come from God and not from governments, the virus's ability to replicate is limited.

---

[3] Pierre Manent, An Intellectual History of Liberalism Princeton University Press. (1994) pp 20–38.

It is no coincidence that the relative dormancy of the progressive virus and the genesis of America took place in roughly the same time frame. America's founders took much of their positive inspiration from Locke, Montesquieu, Voltaire and Hobbes. For example, compare these two passages, one from Thomas Jefferson's contribution to the Declaration of Independence and one from John Locke's Second Essay, published in 1693. First John Locke:

> "Secondly: I answer, such revolutions happen not upon every little mismanagement in public affairs. Great mistakes in the ruling part, many wrong and inconvenient laws, and all the slips of human frailty will be borne by the people without mutiny or murmur. But if a long train of abuses, prevarications, and artifices, all tending the same way, make the design visible to the people, and they cannot but feel what they lie under, and see whither they are going, it is not to be wondered that they should then rouse themselves, and endeavor to put the rule into such hands which may secure to them the end for which government was at first erected..." [4]

---

[4] John Locke. Concerning the true extent and end of civil government. Second Essay, Chapter 19. 1693.

Thomas Jefferson, The Declaration of Independence, 1776:

> "Prudence, indeed, will dictate that Governments long established should not be changed for light and transient causes; and accordingly all experience hath shown, that mankind are more disposed to suffer, while evils are sufferable, than to right themselves by abolishing the forms to which they are accustomed. But when a long train of abuses and usurpations, pursuing invariably the same Object evinces a design to reduce them under absolute Despotism, it is their right, it is their duty, to throw off such Government, and to provide new Guards for their future security." [5]

Later in the 18th century the nascent progressive virus reemerged with the help of Rousseau. He wrote some of the more important code for the virus. Rousseau advocated that citizens and governments should emphasize the collective, not promote individual liberty and freedom. Rousseau argued against a citizen's right to own property. Rousseau supported creating a centralized government with the power to redistribute wealth to achieve collective justice, an early iteration of what would come to be known as "social justice."

---

[5] Thomas Jefferson. Declaration of Independence, 1776.

The dawn of the 19th century ushered in an ever-strengthening virus. August Comte laid the foundation for what would become secular humanism when he created a new religion known as *The Religion of Humanity.* Still, his belief in objective good and bad, along with his desire to live a virtuous life, protected him from many of the debilitating effects of the virus he was helping to create.

The fledgling DNA code of progressivism would eventually be added to and strengthened by Søren Kirkegaard and Friedrich Nietzsche. In a letter written to his friend Peter W. Lund, Kirkegaard exhibited some of the early symptoms of a progressive infection:

> "What I really lack is to be clear in my mind what I am to do, not what I am to know, except in so far as a certain knowledge must precede every action. The thing is to understand myself, to see what God really wishes me to do: the thing is to find a truth which is true for me, to find the idea for which I can live and die. ... I certainly do not deny that I still recognize an imperative of knowledge and that through it one can work upon men, but it must be taken up into my life,

and that is what I now recognize as the most important thing." [6]

Kirkegaard's immune system, weak though it was, protected him from completely succumbing to the ill effects of the virus he was unwittingly helping to create because of his belief in God. Nevertheless, he strengthened that part of the virus that declares *man can create his own truth.*

The 19th Century found a distinct split into two camps, those with immunity to the virus and those who were predisposed to become infected. No one embodies those with immunity better than Alexis de Tocqueville. His masterpiece, *Democracy in America,* stands out as a primer on how to defend against the progressive virus. The book gives testimony to the uniqueness of America's founding principles.

America was founded on principles designed to provide a permanent barrier to an all-powerful central government that was intent upon regulating everything. The British Monarchy was an elitist, top-down power structure that imposed tyranny on the American colonies. The monarchy believed that its will superseded the will of God. The British elites defined reality for the colonies and embodied the very essence of progressivism's totalitarian mandate. It was just short of a miracle that anyone

---

[6] Kierkegaard, Søren. The Essential Kierkegaard, edited by Howard and Edna Hong. Princeton, 2000.

or anything could challenge and then overcome the seemingly invincible British Monarchy. Here is an excerpt from de Tocqueville's *Democracy in America* that captures this miracle:

"Moreover, almost all the sects of the United States are comprised within the great unity of Christianity, and Christian morality is everywhere the same. In the United States the sovereign authority is religious, and consequently hypocrisy must be common; but there is no country in the whole world in which the Christian religion retains a greater influence over the souls of men than in America, and there can be no greater proof of its utility, and of its conformity to human nature, than that its influence is most powerfully felt over the most enlightened and free nation of the earth.

The Americans combine the notions of Christianity and of liberty so intimately in their minds, that it is impossible to make them conceive the one without the other; and with them this conviction does not spring from that barren traditionary faith which seems to vegetate in the soul rather than to live.

There are certain populations in Europe whose unbelief is only equaled by their ignorance and their debasement, while in America one of the freest and most enlightened nations in the world fulfills all the outward duties of religion with fervor.

Upon my arrival in the United States, the religious aspect of the country was the first thing that struck my attention; and the longer I stayed there, the more did I perceive the great political consequences resulting from this state of things, to which I was unaccustomed. In France I had almost always seen the spirit of religion and the spirit of freedom pursuing courses diametrically opposed to each other; but in America I found that they were intimately united, and that they reigned in common over the same country." [7]

With regard to de Tocqueville's reference to the debasement and ignorance found among certain people in Europe, no one person stands out more prominently than Friedrich Nietzsche.

---

[7] Alexis de Tocqueville, Democracy in America,. New York: A. S. Barnes & Co., 1851, pp. 331, 332, 335, 336-7, 337.

Nietzsche strengthened the progressive virus to a new level of virulence in the 19th century. Nietzsche was one of the first to assert that the inequities of man's existence meant that God must be, at least metaphorically, dead. Nietzsche discounted evil as a force that could account for man's bad behavior.

Nietzsche fell victim to the fruits of his labor and developed what we will learn is a hallmark symptom of a progressive infection: flirtation with, if not outright abuse and reliance upon, mind altering substances. By 1882, Nietzsche found himself addicted to opium.[8] Later in his life he began writing his own prescriptions for chloral hydrate, a sedative hypnotic.[9]

The 20th century ushered in a key developer of the progressive virus, Jean Paul Sartre. Sartre stated as fact that a human being, by virtue of his or her consciousness, creates values and determines reality. Sartre personally fell prey to a classic symptom of a progressive infection: a pervasive dissatisfaction with life itself.

Sartre wrote that part of the progressive virus convinces its victim that he can become almost anything, if only he can imagine it and wish it be true.[10] As the idle-rich of the era flirted

---

[8] Cate, Curtis. Friedrich Nietzsche. Woodstock, NY: The Overlook Press, 2005 p.389.
[9] Ibid. p. 453.
[10] Walter Kaufmann, *Existentialism: From Dostoevesky to Sartre*, New York (1956); Guignon, Charles B. and Derk Pereboom. *Existentialism: basic writings* (Hackett Publishing, 2001.

with the progressive virus, more and more of them began to suffer the ill effects of a progressive infection.

Albert Camus was, like Sartre, an early victim whose life became consumed with the progressive virus. Camus represents one of the first men who completely succumbed to a progressive infection. He certainly was not alone, however. Simone de Beauvoir was, like Camus, a victim of the progressive virus who fell completely and irreparably under its spell. Beauvoir was an early feminist and avowed atheist. One only needs to explore the subjects that came to consume Camus and Beauvoir during their lifetime to understand the classic symptoms of a full-blown infection with the progressive virus, e.g., the assumed meaninglessness of life, suicidal thoughts, drug abuse, embracing revolution and the desire to control their fellow man using governmental power.

Camus authored yet another key component of the progressive virus when he developed what came to be known as *The School of Absurdism*. His belief that life is absurd, and his resultant obsession with the absurdity of life, created any number of troubling and ultimately debilitating symptoms for himself and those whom he infected. As Camus developed and shed his virus in his various literary works, his ideas morphed into a "school" of philosophical thought that infected those who became its students.

When Camus wrote *The Myth of Sisyphus* in 1942, he set forth his philosophy of the absurd, and in so doing, wrote that DNA sequence in the progressive virus's code that became one of progressivism's hallmark pathologies:

> Mankind's futile search for meaning, unity and
> clarity in the face of an unintelligible world devoid
> of God and eternal or objective truths or values.

Beauvoir became romantically involved with Sartre. It has been reported that one day while they were sitting on a bench outside the Louvre, he said: "Let's sign a two-year lease." [11] The two never married but were reputed to have an "open" relationship where both experimented with the opposite sex. [12]

Another hallmark symptom of a full-blown progressive infection is its victim's fascination with the meaninglessness of life. The virus creates a distortion of reality that makes its victim believe that any inequity in achievement or outcome, in almost any field or endeavor between groups, is the result of the higher achiever's oppression of the lesser achieved.

As the progressive infection spreads from individual men and women to the culture at large, we begin to see a constellation of symptoms that manifest as an obsession with

---

[11] Bair, Deidre. A biography of Simon de Beauvoir. Touchstone publishing, 1991.

[12] Appignanesi, Lisa (10 June 2005). "Our relationship was the greatest achievement of my life". The Guardian (London).

and attraction to Marxism, Communism and all things related to socialism in its various forms. The natural progression of the infection begins with veiled liberalism, followed by progressivism, evolving into socialism, then communism, then spiraling into absolute tyranny.

This natural progression of the disease is seen very clearly in the life and times of Camus who, as a young man, was a "nice" liberal thinker. Later in his life, however, Camus's infection pressured him to join the French Communist Party in the spring of 1935. The virus had implored him to remedy the perceived inequalities, that is, restore social justice, between Europeans and natural born Algerians.

In 1936 Camus joined the activities of the Algerian People's Party (Le Parti du Peuple Algérien). As the virus festered, Camus went on to join the French anarchist movement. Camus's movement toward anarchism represents one of the first illustrations of a classic pattern in the virus's mode of operation:

> Embracing socialism is a characteristic of the optimistic side of the progressive victim's clinical presentation while embracing anarchy reflects the victims almost inevitable spiraling down into a vacuous chasm of anger and despair.

> When progressives feel there is some hope to achieving social justice, they embrace socialism.

However, when the virus flares up, the patient will quickly sink into despair. Absent a reprieve from that despair, the progressive victim will embrace anarchy. As the progressive infection waxes and wanes between adopting socialism and anarchy, thoughts of and fascination with suicide are ever-present.

In 1934, Camus married Simone Hie, a morphine addict and the daughter of a wealthy ophthalmologist. Here we see demonstrated a fundamental truth in the development of the progressive's disease. Freedom from worrying about material survival exacerbates the infection. Marrying money inflamed the viral infection plaguing Camus.

After a year or so the marriage ended as a consequence of infidelities on both sides. In 1940, Camus married Francine Faure, a socialite pianist and mathematician. In a classic symptom display of the virus infecting his mind, Camus railed against marriage while going through the motions of committing to the institution. Camus and his wife gave birth to twin girls in 1945. It was widely known at the time that even with a wife and two small children at home, Camus conducted numerous affairs, including a notoriously public affair with the Spanish-born actress Maria Casares. [13]

---

[13] Lennon, Peter *Camus and His Women*. Guardian. 1997-10-15).

Camus possessed a fledging awareness of the infection that was consuming his life. In fact, Camus described his belief system as a "philosophical suicide."

> "I call the existential attitude philosophical suicide. How else to start from the world's lack of meaning and end up by finding a meaning and a depth to it?" [14]

When Camus referenced "finding meaning and depth," he was referring to the poisonous meaning and depth that comes from the submission to the vacuum of meaninglessness.

> Thus, it is the acceptance of the meaninglessness of life that ultimately has any meaning whatsoever for the infected. The infected is left with a vacuous sense of meaning that is rooted to nothingness. Like the man adrift on the open ocean, "water, water, everywhere and not a drop to drink," those infected with the progressive virus are perpetually conflicted and awash in a sea of nothingness.
>
> ***But for their self-indulgent obsession with their taste buds, adolescent-like sexuality and their angry and obsessive need to control and***

---

[14] Appignanesi, Richard *Introducing Existentialism*; Totem. 1998, p. 36.

regulate others in service to social justice, progressives would have nothing to live for.

The reader should understand that the progressive virus nullifies the quest for objective truth and the achievement of virtue. The progressive virus replaces truth and virtue with an obsession with self, relativistic values, the rejection of rooted biological and cultural differences between individuals and groups and, most importantly, a rejection of God.

The progressive epidemic changed everything that preceded it in the same way that a computer infected with a malware virus never acts or behaves the same. The keyboard entry "a" may become an "o." Paragraphs may be juxtaposed and pieced into other word processing documents and system crashes come unexpectedly.

Before the appearance of the progressive virus, man accepted as true that the highest ethical good is the same for everyone and that good has an objective quality to it. The quest for absolute truth and the nobility of man was transformed once the progressive virus began to make inroads in the culture.

It would be easy to conclude that progressivism is but a version of existentialism, but that is not true. The existentialist movement did, however, create a nurturing environment for the development of the progressive virus. Camus was smart enough to know that whatever had infected him was distinct from the philosophy to which he is most closely associated, i.e., existentialism. If we characterize existentialism as a common cold, then being infected with the progressive virus is tantamount to contracting a virulent case of pneumonia.

Camus did not consider himself to be an existentialist. His fledgling awareness that his was a unique condition, related to but distinct from existentialism, illustrates that he understood that he was suffering from something unique. Camus declared this:

> "No, I am not an existentialist. Sartre and I are always surprised to see our names linked. We have even thought of publishing a short statement in which the undersigned declare that they have nothing in common with each other and refuse to be held responsible for the debts they might respectively incur. It's a joke actually. Sartre and I published our books without exception before we had ever met. When we did get to know each other, it was to realize how much we differed. Sartre is an existentialist, and the only book of ideas that I have published, The Myth of Sisyphus, was directed

against   the   so-called   existentialist
philosophers."[15]

The progressive virus, like any infective agent, must reach a critical biological mass before it can shed its way into creating an epidemic in the culture at large. It would take the nascent communications revolution of the 1920s, followed by another viral outbreak in the 1960s, before progressivism would reach a critical biological mass.

In the early part of the twentieth century, the progressive virus was recognized for its potential use by revolutionaries in their efforts to control their fellow citizens.

Revolutionaries recognized that citizens infected with the progressive virus would not only allow them to exercise confiscatory power, but would welcome their creation of an ever encroaching central government. All that was needed was for revolutionaries to convince the public infected with the virus that their motivation to confiscate and redistribute wealth derived from their desire to achieve "fairness" and social justice.

All societies and cultures are heterogeneous mixtures of people with differing levels of talent, skills, industry, motivation and opportunity. However, if men and women are presumed to be born as a blank slate, if they are "made" by their

---

[15] From An interview with Jeanine Delpech, in Les Nouvelles Littéraires, 1945. Cited in Albert Camus: Lyrical and Critical Essays, Vintage, 1970.

environment, as the progressive virus declares, then the fact that some people are more successful or possess more wealth than others must mean that the successful oppressed the not so successful. It means that social injustice in one citizen's environment "created" the inequity in outcome. Inequality, when you believe that it derives from the haves oppressing the have-nots, encourages the desire to confiscate and redistribute material wealth. It means that equal opportunity is replaced with a focus upon equal outcomes.

A progressive infection creates a sense of entitlement among the have-nots, favors the displacement of responsibility to others or the culture at large for one's fate, and creates a citizen that dreams of and expects grand success absent effort, talent or dedication. If that entitlement-minded citizen is taught to believe that he is destined to be great, but then fails to achieve great wealth and success as he or she matures, then these victims of the virus conclude that they must have been oppressed or deprived. Average people, by virtue of being simply average and being infected with the progressive virus, become chronically dissatisfied with being average and blame their resultant unhappiness on those more successful.

The first widespread epidemic of the progressive virus manifested in the United States as the "Roaring Twenties." The symptoms of Hedonism, self-indulgence, gin-filled bathtubs and promiscuity infected much of the population in large cities.

Nevertheless, the Roaring Twenties never fully consumed the culture at large because of the remnants of the preceding culture's emphasis upon virtue. This was true for even those gin-soaked flappers who, once they got older, regretted what they often referred to as a fall from grace. Here is one description of the 1920s that captures the flavor of the time:

> "In America, a flapper has always been a giddy, attractive and slightly unconventional young thing who, in [H. L.] Mencken's words, 'was a somewhat foolish girl, full of wild surmises and inclined to revolt against the precepts and admonitions of her elders.'[16] During the 1920s the population in cities rapidly grew. Crime and political corruption became common and acceptable. Following a relatively conservative period following the First World War, liberalism began to spread throughout urban areas during the years following 1925. Urban areas began to hold increasingly liberal views of sex, alcohol, drugs, and homosexuality. The view that women

---

[16] Andrist, Ralph. *The American Heritage: History of the 20s and 30s.* New York: American Heritage Publishing Company, 1970.

and minorities were entitled to equality in outcome became increasingly prevalent in urban areas, especially among those steeped in progressive thought. For example, the actor William Haines, who was regularly named in newspapers and magazines as the #1 male box-office draw, openly lived in a gay relationship with his lover Jimmie Shields. Many people in rural areas became increasingly shocked at all the changes they saw occurring and many responded by becoming reactionary. The Volstead Act, a law meant to uphold the Eighteenth Amendment, was difficult due to lack of funding, short staffing and a disregard and disdain for a law that was deemed ridiculous. The fact that members of congress became drunk from toasts after passing the Eighteenth Amendment reveals that even those who were supposed to be setting an example did not take the law seriously. This lack of respect for the law enforcement eventually spread to other areas of culture, and many conservative members of the United States

Congress criticized this lack of order as stemming from the rampant use of alcohol. " [17]

Ever since the initial outbreak of progressivism in 1920s America, a series of ever more virulent epidemics have occurred. Most notably, the 1960s epidemic stands out because it was the first time progressivism was able to reach a critical mass that virtually insured future generations would be infected by the virus.

The progressive virus prays upon youthful optimism and gullibility. During the decade of 1960 to 1969, 70 million adolescents came of age, the result of the post WWII baby boom. The 60s generation was the most pampered and self-indulged group of Americans who had ever lived.

Their parents, many of whom survived the depression of the 1930s and lived through WWII, made sure their children had anything and everything they did not have. Their children were raised to believe that they were the center of the universe. Books on raising children that stressed permissive and self-indulgence replaced discipline, frugality and personal responsibility.

Benjamin Spock's book: "The Common Sense Book of Baby and Child Care," published in 1946, became the bible of child

---

[17] Lambert M Surhone, Miriam T Timpledon, Susan F Marseken. Social Issues of the 1920s. VDM Verlag Dr. Mueller AG & Co. Kg, Jul 2, 2010.

rearing for many baby boomer parents. That book was a progressive's dream come true as it codified, under the authority of a doctor, relativistic values and provided a primer on what may as well have been a "how to book" on how to raise a child so that he is more likely to develop a narcissistic personality disorder.

Other books impregnated with the progressive virus both reflected the changing times and helped to promote progressive dogma, these included: *The Silent Spring*, written by Rachel Carson, *The Games People Play*, written by Eric Berne, *Valley of the Dolls*, written by Jacqueline Susann and *The Feminine Mystique*, written by Betty Friedan.

In Friedan's book, she defined "mystique" as the worthlessness women supposedly feel in roles that require them to be financially, intellectually and emotionally dependent upon their husbands. Friedan went on to assert that women are victims of a false belief system that requires them to find identity and meaning in their lives through their husbands and children.

In *The Silent Spring*, Carson concluded that DDT and other pesticides had irrevocably harmed birds and animals and had contaminated the entire world food supply. In one chapter of her book "A Fable for Tomorrow," Carson depicted a nameless American town where all life, including fish, birds, fruit trees and all the town's children had been "silenced" by the insidious effects of DDT.

In *Valley of the Dolls*, which sold over 30 million copies, Susann chronicles the lives of three young women who claw and fight their way to fame and fortune while fighting their addiction to "dolls," another name for pills and drugs.

In *Games People Play*, psychiatrist and transactional analyst Eric Berne framed human interaction as an exchange and bartering of selfish wants and needs between two players. Altruism was discounted as nothing more than an artificial construct in service to self-interest.

Timothy Leary helped to spread the progressive virus to an entire generation. Leary's progressive mantra of "tune in, turn on, and drop out" became the mantra of many unsuspecting children of the 1960s. When Leary popularized LSD he was simply reinforcing Descarte's "Je pense donc je suis," through the neuro-distortions created by hallucinogenic drugs.

Cultural events of the 1960s were misinterpreted as confirming key assumptions of progressive dogma. John and Robert Kennedy's assassination, along with the assassination of Martin Luther King, seemed to reinforce the notion of the ultimate futility of life itself. The Viet Nam war seemed to confirm the cynicism of people who were told that their government was acting in good faith for noble purposes.

Viet Nam's influence was profound on the children coming of age in the 1960s. The war wasn't good and it wasn't noble, not because people in authority misrepresented what was good and noble, although that too, but because the war removed that last bit of immunity fending off the virus's insistence that there is no "good" and there is no "noble."

As if to dot the "i", the Watergate affair in the early 1970s reinforced progressive's belief in the mercurial quality of values. Watergate also set the stage for the metamorphosis of the American press from objectivity to involvement with a vested interest in the outcome of whatever it was covering. Woodward and Bernstein of the Washington Post motivated an entire generation of journalists who would reject objectivity and replace it with a vested interest in the outcome of the subject of their coverage.

Just as objective truths were rejected, out of hand, by progressives, so it was that objective journalism, as a paradigm, was also rejected. As journalists infected with the progressive virus entered the work force, they brought with them their progressive distortions. While some journalists give lip-service to objectivity, the fact of the matter is today's journalists, as a whole, are emotionally involved, vested in and impregnate any story with their own, personal truths. The choice of what to publish, the angle of approach to the story, the words chosen, the selection of accompanying photos and illustrations, *reflect someone's desire to create an effect in the reader or viewer, and do not reflect a desire or intent to capture objectivity.*

Objectivity, as a journalistic paradigm, has been discarded as an outdated and invalid approach to reportage. As schools of journalism attracted those infected with the progressive virus, while at the same time deselecting those aspiring journalists who were immune to the virus, the profession became an advocate for all things progressive and a motivated detractor of traditional America.

Journalists found no need to conspire or compare notes with their colleagues; it wasn't necessary. This is because the vast majority of journalists are like-minded. MSNBC.com looked at the political contributions of 143 journalists from 2004 to the start of the 2008 presidential campaign. What they found is not surprising. Of the 143 journalists studied, 123 gave money to Democrats or liberal candidates. Only 16 journalists donated to Republican candidates, with two giving to both parties.[18] Schools of journalism hone their student's progressive predispositions and have been successful at creating a "Fourth Estate" that is

---

[18] NBC News.com. Bill Dedman, Investigative reporter. June 25, 2007.

little more than a political action committee whose credo is: "The end justifies the means."

The media's bias has not fallen on deaf ears. In September of 2011, the Pew Research Center published its findings on the American public's view of the media. [19] The center's research spanned the years 1985 to 2011. Among the center's findings: 63% of Americans say that they want news coverage with no particular point of view, i.e., they want objective news reporting. 66% of respondents stated that news stories are inaccurate. 77% think that news organizations favor one side over the other and 80% believe that news outlets, and their reporters, are influenced by powerful people and organizations.

The findings were not limited to the national press. As "happy news" became the standard for local news, the public's distrust skyrocketed. Fully 69% of respondents stated that they had lost some trust in local news organizations.

In 1985, 34% of Americans believed that the press dealt fairly with candidates from the major parties. That number shrank to only 16% in 2011. In 1985, 53% of Americans stated that the press tended to favor one party's candidate over his opponent. In 2011 that number had increased to a whopping 77%.

---

[19] Pew Research Center for the People and the Press. *Views of the Media, 1985-2011.* September 22, 2011.

The progressive virus has permeated much of the media since the 1960s. The press, like any victim of the virus, has become weakened and is at risk for losing what waning credibility it once had. The power the press wields with such bias and arrogant surety is waning. Ironically, the press is being systematically destroyed by the very virus it embraces.

CHAPTER TWO

Progressive Entrepreneurs

ONCE IT BECAME WIDELY accepted that virtue and truths were merely reference points along man's every changing perceptual terrain, it dawned on psychologists and would-be-psychologist entrepreneurs that the vacuum in meaning created by the progressive virus could be filled with humanistic protocols for living, that is, for a price. Any number of humanistic entrepreneurs packaged and sold the progressive virus in the decades that followed the 1960s.

In the 1960s a former used car salesman by the name of Jack Rosenberg dumped his wife and four children and changed his name to Werner Hans Erhard. He moved to California and started a company named "EST." Erhard was one of the first to create a poisonous vaccine infected with a nearly complete and fully functional progressive virus.

EST seminars emphasized self-focus and the manipulation of what had previously been known as values and guilt. Erhard promised self-fulfillment through the exploration of "possibilities," which was a euphemism for a central tenet of progressivism that a seminar participant could re-write his life, with an emphasis upon removing guilt. A key component of Erhard's seminar was learning to control others through manipulation in service to getting what you wanted.

> "The training sessions offered by EST became notorious for their rigid discipline – trainees were forbidden to go to the lavatory or speak to each other during sessions – using a confrontational approach. EST courses usually took place on two consecutive weekends, with trainees being expected to explore life's possibilities, under intense and sometimes bullying scrutiny from trainers, for as much as 15 hours a day." [20]

"The 1990s saw Erhard's empire begin to disintegrate. He went through a contentious divorce from his second wife who stated that his "ego and public image are the most important things in the world to him." In 1991, several former employees brought lawsuits, charging Erhard with crimes ranging from fraud to physical abuse, all of which Erhard denied." [21]

---

[20] Ben Macintyre. The London Times, July 22, 1992.
[21] Ibid.

According to a CBS News 60 Minutes exposé on Erhard, Bob Larzelere, a chief trainer of EST, said that Erhard declared himself to be God during staff meetings. [22]

> The progressive virus creates this tendency for man to think of himself as God because the virus destroys God but not the need of man to fill the vacuum created when man rejects the existence of God.

Erhard preyed upon the 60s generation and their progeny who had been stripped of many of their meaning anchors by virtue of their infection with the progressive virus. Erhard packaged and sold a fully functional form of the progressive virus. EST provided a method to brainwash away virtues in favor of a rampant narcissism that was solely concerned with feeling good absent guilt and moral obligations.

As the progressive virus replicated, those carrying the virus infiltrated educational institutions, social networks and government bureaucracies. The progressive virus is easily packaged within virtually all forms of media, that is, virus infected information.

By the 1980s the virus became so widespread its early genetic engineers simply sat back and watched the epidemic unfold before their eyes. The so-called *Me Generation* had been

---

[22] CBS News, "60 Minutes." August 26, 2009.

so universally infected that only a few among them could recognize that something was terribly wrong. Just like the members of a leper colony who had never laid eyes on a non-infected person, sickness with the progressive virus became the new normal.

Once enough citizens had been infected, progressive-influenced bureaucracies were created by politicians, and their financiers, with little opposition from the public who had become immuno-compromised. Once the mass media became infiltrated with those carrying the progressive virus, the mind control crowd, like the virus that has successfully infiltrated a host cell, became nothing more than a virus generator. As progressives infiltrated society's most influential institutions, the viral epidemic consumed the country.

CHAPTER THREE

The Progressive Virus Infiltrates the Government

BY THE 1980s EST and its successor psychobabble-based seminars had made their way into America's most important federal agencies. A man by the name of Gregory May, aka Gregory May and Associates (GMA), provided progressive infected seminars to federal employees beginning in 1984.

In a matter brought by federal prosecutors to enforce a subpoena against May, the Ninth Circuit Court of Appeal wrote:

> "The subpoena enforcement action was brought by the Department of Transportation's ("DOT") Inspector General ("IG") in connection with an investigation of contracts between DOT and GMA. GMA is a psychological corporation that provides training workshops to institutional and personal clients. GMA has provided various management-training courses to the United States DOT since 1984. From 1986 through April, 1993, GMA received more than 200 direct procurements totaling more than **$41.4 million**

from DOT for training programs to the Federal
Aviation Administration ("FAA")." [23]

In 1995 before a House of Representative's Subcommittee on Appropriations, a witness by the name of Stephen Pressman testified on the subject of new age seminars, paid for by the American taxpayer to the tune of **$41.4 million dollars**. The Honorable Frank Wolf Chairman, Subcommittee on Science, State, Justice, and Commerce, and Related Agencies Committee on Appropriations, conducted the questioning:

Mr. WOLF. Would you describe "EST" and tell us Gregory May's association with it?

> "EST refers to "Erhard Seminar Training," and was
> founded by Werner Erhard. EST has gone through
> various corporate identities and the training is
> now conducted by an organization known as
> Landmark Education. The EST organization
> conducted seminars for individuals and also
> developed corporate training, first through
> Werner Erhard and Associates and later through a
> company known as Transformational
> Technologies. The individual training is now
> referred to as The Forum. EST seminars have

---

[23] UNITED STATES of America, Plaintiff-Appellee, v. GREGORY MAY & ASSOCIATES, Defendant-Appellant. 41 F.3d 1514, No. 94-15972. Ninth Circuit. Submitted Sept. 15, 1994, Decided Nov. 9, 1994.

been widely publicized in the media. Our investigation did not include an in depth examination of EST beyond media reports. We consulted with a New Age Training consultant, however, who was himself an EST graduate. This expert conducted an analysis which drew several parallels between GMA and EST training." [24]

Later in the hearing yet another reveal occurred that illustrates the progressive's confusion over the meaning of controlling other people by exploiting their progressive illness:

"We also spoke to a number of witnesses who commented on the relationship between Gregory May and the FAA Human Resources staff. One witness stated that Gregory May was considered "God," and another stated that Gregory May was viewed as the "second coming of Christ" within Human Resources."

Is it any wonder that those afflicted with the progressive virus, and who also run segments of or influence governmental power, come to view themselves as god-like? Unfortunately they are not, as history teaches us, benevolent gods, but rather, gods

---

[24] Department of Transportation and Related Agencies Appropriations for 1996, Hearings Before a Subcommittee of the Committee on Appropriations, House of Representatives, ISBN 0160473527 , Page 834-835, 104th Congress, 1st Session, 1995.

who invariably impose tyranny upon as many people as they can manage to control through the imposition of regulations, taxes and the empowerment of intrusive bureaucrats that rule every aspect of a citizen's life.

Progressive infected training organizations have cropped up everywhere, ready to provide to government employees and union members exposure to the progressive virus. One such organization is the wholesome sounding Midwest Academy. Here is what the Academy says about itself:

> "The Midwest Academy is a national training institute committed to advancing the struggle for social, economic, and racial justice. From local neighborhood groups to statewide and national organizations, Midwest Academy has trained over twenty-five thousand grassroots activists from hundreds of organizations and coalitions. Midwest Academy teaches an organizing philosophy, methods and skills that enable ordinary people to actively participate in the democratic process. Courses and consulting services are designed for progressive organizations and coalitions that utilize civic

engagement activities to build citizen power at all levels of our democracy." [25]

The Midwest Academy was founded in 1973 by Heather Booth and her husband Paul. Paul Booth was a founder and former National Secretary of Students for a Democratic Society (SDS), an early virus generator steeped in anarchist ambition. Paul was also the former President of Chicago's Citizen Action Program (CAP), formed in 1969 by trainees from Saul Alinsky's Industrial Areas Foundation (IAF). Mr. Booth is currently an assistant to Gerald McEntee. McEntee is President of the American Federation of State, County and Municipal Employees (AFSCME), a public employees union.

Among the student population of the Midwest Academy is the AFL/CIO labor union. The "Union Summer" training camp infected thousands of labor organizers with the progressive virus, with an emphasis upon "Direct Action," i.e., *the use of confrontation and intimidation to get what you want.* It should come as no surprise that one prominent Midwest Academy graduate is Service Employees International Union (SEIU) President Andrew Stern.

The Midwest Training Academy has not been shy when it comes to influencing elections in the United States. In 1993 Heather Booth became Training Director for the Democratic

---

[25] http://www.Midwestacademy.com/about-us.

National Committee. Donations to the DNC funded Booth's training. In this job she solicited endorsements for President Bill Clinton's policies from a wide array of interest groups. In 1992 Booth directed the Field Operation for Illinois Democrat Carol Moseley Braun's successful run for the U.S. Senate. Booth also served as a legislative aide to Democratic Senator Howard Metzenbaum before he retired in 1995.

The Academy's influence didn't stop there. Heather Booth was the founding director of the NAACP National Voter Fund in 2000. Through her efforts she helped to increase African American voter turnout by nearly 2 million votes. She has provided training to a variety of social change groups including the Center for Community Change, with an emphasis upon getting the vote out, and Move-On.org. Heather Booth is deeply involved in the promotion of multiculturalism. Her efforts on behalf of The Campaign for Comprehensive Immigration Reform seek to open the borders of the United States and give blanket amnesty to the unscreened illegal immigrants currently living in America, while providing ever-increasing taxpayer funded assistance to illegal immigrants. Booth has taught the principles of progressivism to The Campaign for America's Future and the National Organization of Women. Each of these groups is a progressive virus generator dedicated to social engineering. The success of these groups can be measured by the fact that the progressive infection has reached the very top of the political food chain.

President Bill Clinton exhibited many symptoms of a progressive infection, including an attraction to purveyors of EST-like dogma. The fact that Clinton was both a victim and advocate of the progressive virus meant that rather than turn to God, or rely upon core values when under stress, Clinton tended to reach out to new age gurus whose stock in trade is reinforcement of the basic tenets of progressivism.

Those tenets in practice include the promotion of self-affirmation, high self-esteem paired with the mitigation of the remnants of guilt and remorse via confrontational methods. The "patient" feels better, but only for a time.

In 1994 Clinton reached out to Anthony Jay Mahavorick, aka Tony Robbins. Robbins is a high school graduate who became expert at disseminating the progressive virus in the form of seminars and audio recordings that emphasized personal wealth, social dominance and the absence of guilt.

Robbins was an early "fire walker" who took advantage of his follower's ignorance on the subject of heat conduction. Robbins brainwashed his unsuspecting believers into concluding that after listening to him, and focusing upon self, one could walk across glowing embers without getting burned.

Robbins also traded in neuorlinguistic programming (NLP) a discredited pseudo-science that used a self-delusional mantra not unlike the delusions believed to be real by schizophrenics. With regard to NLP, scientific reviews of NLP have been unforgiving. Beyerstein, for instance, has labeled NLP a total con and nothing but new-age fakery. [26]

In a telling entry in his personal diary, written in 2004, Clinton exhibited virtually all of the classic symptoms of a progressive infection. One symptom, "the emptiness of life" was the heading Clinton gave to his diary entry. In that diary entry the former president talks about seeking help for his sickness from none other than Tony Robbins.

"FRIDAY, JULY 09, 2004

Tony Robbins and Emptiness in Life

I'm feeling much better today. Strange how getting the message that my books aren't selling can set me off like that. After all those years of political strife, I'm still sensitive about what people think about me.

I called Tony Robbins, a very good friend of mine and what most people call a mental guru. During

---

[26] Beyerstein.B.L (1990). "Brainscams: Neuromythologies of the New Age." International Journal of Mental Health 19(3): 27-36,27.

my impeachment predicament he helped me through some of my most difficult moments. Every time I thought "give up, it's not worth it" he was there to talk to me, to coach me and to push me to keep on keeping on. A big part of the reason I got through the affair was his help.

We talked for about two hours. He's still as sharp as he ever was. He straightened me out pretty good. What he said to me is confrontational, but true. I know it is true.

He said I fear an impartial judgment of my life's work, my 8 years as president. He said that is the reason I fear the drop in sales of my book. He said that was the reason I fear Kerry winning the presidency.

Till now, he said, I personified the Democratic party and the liberal movement. He said, if Kerry wins the election, he will personify the Democratic party and the liberal movement.

Till now Democrats and liberals defended me and my record, because they saw an attack on me and my record as an attack on the Democratic party and liberalism by fundamentalist Christian and conservative forces.

What will happen if I'm not the personification of the progressive movement in this country? Will my presidency lose its luster? Will they reappraise it? Will I become another president Carter, who's only remembered for the Iran Hostage debacle? Will a lifetime of hard work be reduced to "that president with that intern"?

The reappraisal has started. I've sold about 4 million books. That's a lot and I thank each and every one, who bought the book. But Outkast, the rapper has sold many more CDs. More people went to see "Mean Girls".

How did the critics rate my book? They hated it. They thought it was rubbish. Some said so without reading the book. I mean how can you read 650 pages, which took me 3 years to write in 24 hours?

I feel like my time is over. My shine is gone. The Teflon is gone. I'm just a citizen. I used to be big. I used to be loved or hated. I used to be somebody. Somebody, who mattered.

Tony said, Tony Robbins, not the British prime minister, he said I need to deal with this. I can't do anything about people's perception of my presidency. I can't stop progress in the Democratic Party. New people will have to man the top positions.

He told me to move on with my life. Do I have a life? Apart from the politician Bill Clinton? I have Chelsea and Hillary. Chelsea is all grown up. She has her own life. Hillary has her own life too. Separate from me. She is a senator for New York State. I used to have a lot of supporters, but the sales of my book and the criticism I got shows me I'm on the way out. My supporters will soon be

President Kerry and Vice President Edwards supporters.

Who am I if not the politician Bill Clinton? Ever since my first election in the early seventies, I've been Bill Clinton the politician. Thinking about it right now, I know I'm nothing else but a politician. I feel pretty lonely. With all my friends, my supporters, Hillary and Chelsea, I feel all alone, because all these people are connected with the politician Bill Clinton, not with me personally. How many friends do I have? How many people like me?

Tony Robbins is right. It's over. I need to put politics behind me. Problem is, I am politics. I have never nurtured anything else but the politician in me. If I have to move on, I'll have to start from scratch.

All of a sudden, I'm 57 and I'm nobody and I have nobody. When I look around right now, I see the security guard leaning back in his chair. He notices me and gives me a disinterested look back. I see the housekeeper cleaning the window. The look on her face tells me she'd rather be somewhere else. I see the spots she left on the window. I know I'll have to talk to her about her work pretty soon and I know she's so beaten by decades of hard manual labor, she won't even care if I fire her or not. And I look at Bobbi typing away on her notebook. She looks up, gives me one of her big Southern smiles and continues her work.

That's my life when I'm not a politician. The life of Citizen Clinton. Nothing to be proud of."
POSTED BY BILL CLINTON AT 5:33 PM

This diary entry is tantamount to a checklist of the symptoms associated with a progressive infection. Notice that Clinton is self-absorbed and expresses both in the title of his diary entry and in the body of his entry the progressive victim's inevitable battle with despair that comes from having no foundational values, no virtue and no internal compass. Clinton's internal compass is an ever-spinning dial that points in the most expedient and self-serving direction at any given time.

The moral relativism of Bill Clinton is on display for all to see when he writes:

"During my impeachment predicament he (meaning Tony Robbins) helped me through some of my most difficult moments. Every time I thought "give up, it's not worth it" he was there to talk to me, to coach me and to push me to keep on keeping on. A big part of the reason I got through the affair with his help."

The only "affair" Clinton expressed concern about in this diary entry is the impeachment "affair" which began after he was caught committing adultery in the White House with one of his interns, then lying about the matter with a finger-wagging straight face using all the Southern charm he could muster, "I did not have sexual relations with that woman." Guilt over his "affair" with Monica Lewinsky didn't even register during this Diary entry.

(*Said with finger-wagging self-righteousness*) "Now, I have to go back to work on my State of the Union speech. And I worked on it until pretty late last night. But I want to say one thing to the American people. I want you to listen to me. I'm going to say this again: I did not have sexual relations with that woman, Miss Lewinsky. I never told anybody to lie, not a single time; never.

These allegations are false. And I need to go back

to work for the American people. Thank you." [27]

One cannot help but conclude that those moments during his impeachment drama wherein Mr. Clinton felt some guilt, a remnant of not being raised as a progressive, was nullified in short order by Robbins who used techniques that work with those absent a moral compass, these included confrontation and the reinforcement of narcissistic tendencies with self-affirmations. It was Robbins who filled the vacuum in Clinton's psyche, not God, what Clinton's mother had taught him as a child or what noble and honorable men should do when they fall from grace. It is fascinating and very telling that Clinton reached out to Robbins when confronted with a presidential and personal crisis.

Robbins, like Erhard, stripped themselves of their prior identity as easily as changing their underwear. Besides changing their names, they divorced and anointed themselves to be "mental experts." Both men are remarkable in the fact that:

Neither Robbins nor Erhard was successful in any life's endeavor other than purveying their progressive dogma. Imagine a major league pitching coach who never pitched in, or for that

---

[27] University of Virginia. Miller Center. *Response to the Lewinsky Allegations*, January 26, 1998.

matter, played in the major leagues, and you have Tony Robbins, Werner Erhard and a host of other purveyors of the progressive virus.

CHAPTER FOUR

Psychology

IT WASN'T JUST THE pseudo-psychologist entrepreneurs who jumped on the progressive bandwagon. An entire generation of students of psychology, clinical psychologists and psychiatrists have been steeped in progressive dogma. Humanistic, Self-Psychology and Gestalt psychology became formal carriers of the progressive virus.

The Humanistic, Self-Psychology and Gestalt movements came of age in the late 1960s and live to this day. These movements have spread the progressive virus to three generations of Americans. Abraham Maslow, Ph.D., Carl Rogers, Ph.D., Charles Coulson, Ph.D. and Fritz Perls, M.D. were core advocates of and purveyors of the progressive virus.

What is remarkable, and very telling, is that three of the four men (Fritz Perls being the exception), ultimately recanted and summarily rejected the progressive dogma they promoted. In essence, their immune systems managed to fight off the virus that infected them for much of their lives. The millions of students, patients and institutions they infected have not been so fortunate, however.

Maslow's claim to fame was his "self-actualization" thesis. Taking a chapter right out of Jean Paul Sartre's quest for self-indulgence absent guilt, Maslow defined self-actualization as "the desire to become more and more of what one is, to become everything that one is capable of becoming."[28]

Maslow's self-actualization was often used as a means to increase power over others. It was used to justify a rabid self-obsession about feeling good and reaching for what Maslow termed peak experiences. To his credit, Maslow attempted to reign in the virus he so effectively spread at the end of his life.

Later in life, Maslow lamented over-promoting self-actualization. He encouraged his students at Brandeis to return to intellectually more viable pursuits other than the quest for self-actualization and its goal of finding peak experiences.[29] Just before his death, Maslow commented on the severe authority crisis pervading all institutions, He said:

> "[P]articularly intellectuals, must remain ambivalent about power whoever wields it, even

---

[28] Maslow, Abraham. Motivation and personality. Harper and Row New York, New York 1954 pg. 92.

[29] Lowry, Richard J., Ed. (1979). The Journals of A.H. Maslow.

(and especially) when they themselves have authority." [30]

Authority and power were the birthright of those who had achieved self-actualization. What Maslow had not factored into the equation was that then, as now, absolute power corrupts absolutely.

In an earlier May 28, 1967 journal entry Maslow said this about self-actualization: "Self-actualization? I realized I'd rather leave it behind me. Just too sloppy...going through my notes brought this unease to consciousness. It's been with me for years. Meant to write and publish a self-actualization critique, but somehow never did."[31] Maslow privately admitted he had conflated goodness with being self-actualized by "smuggling in" or reducing "ethics" to being characteristic of the healthiest, most self-actualized people. He feared that his friend and colleague, Carl Rogers, was in the grip of 'democratic dogma'. [32] His fear was well founded.

Carl Rogers was responsible for the codification of a key element of the progressive virus, his "person-centered approach" infected psychotherapy, counseling, public school

---

[30] Maslow, Abraham H. (1970). Motivation & Personality, 2nd. Ed. (see preface) New York: Harper.
[31] Lowry, Richard J., Ed. (1979). *The Journals of A.H. Maslow.* pp. 794-795 (also pp. 117-118, 188, 190, 755-56, 832, 848). Monterey, CA: Brooks/Cole.
[32] Ibid. pp. 794-795; 117-118, 188, 190, 755-56, 832, 848). Note: By "democratic dogma," Maslow was referencing the dogma of progressivism.

education, along with numerous bureaucracies within the United States government. Rogers was found to be among the six most eminent psychologists of the 20th century and second, among clinicians, only to Sigmund Freud. [33]

A more mature Carl Rogers, like Maslow, lamented over the fact that his students had adopted his secular edicts on human behavior with "an almost paranoid certainty of their own absolute virtues and correctness." [34] Challenging a key precept of the progressive virus he helped to develop,

> Rogers said that he had **underestimated the power of evil** and downplayed the importance of tradition, authority structures, community and the importance of delaying immediate gratification, etc.[35] (Emphasis added)

No one touted the progressive virus more than Fritz Perls, M.D. He was responsible for foisting upon three generations of unwitting Americans what he termed Gestalt therapy. Gestalt therapy codified what other progressives had only alluded to, the entitlement of self. Perls developed a method to achieving self-obsession. The core of the Gestalt Therapy process is enhanced awareness of sensation, perception, bodily feelings,

---

[33] Haggbloom, S.J. et al. (2002). The 100 Most Eminent Psychologists of the 20th Century. Review of General Psychology. Vol. 6, No. 2, 139–152.

[34] Lowry, Richard J., Ed. (1979). The Journals of A.H. Maslow.

[35] Lowry, Richard J., Ed. (1979). The Journals of A.H. Maslow. 117-118, 188, 190, 755-56, 832, 848). Monterey, CA: Brooks/Cole.

emotion and behavior in the present moment. "How do you feel right now" became the question psychiatrists and psychologists asked with monotonous repetition.

Students, clients and patients were encouraged to attune themselves to each and every little change in bodily sensation. Patients, clients and students already primed to develop a narcissistic personality disorder were encouraged to carry with them at all times a psychological mirror into which they could gaze and see the most important person on the planet Earth-- themselves.

Nothing embodies Perl's Gestalt virus like his "Gestalt Prayer." By calling it a "prayer" he diminished God and simultaneously filled the vacuum he created with the sights, self- smells, wants, wishes and feelings of the Gestalt practitioner. If we were talking about Fritz Perl's having a bad case of the flu, as opposed to his infection with the progressive virus, Perl's "prayer" would be nothing more than a runny nose, high fever and a hacking cough.

"I do my thing and you do your thing.

I am not in this world to live up to your expectations,

And you are not in this world to live up to mine.

You are you, and I am I,

and if by chance we find each other, it's beautiful.

If not, it can't be helped." [36]

When it comes to understanding the virulence of the progressive virus, Charles Coulson, Ph.D. is expert. Coulson is interesting because he was a disciple of Carl Rogers who, along with his mentor, championed the progressive virus in the form of Person-Centered Psychology. Coulson helped to augment the progressive virus with a virulent addition known as the "Encounter-Group." Coulson, perhaps more than any other purveyor of the progressive virus, came to understand the destructive impact progressivism has on people and society.

As a student of Coulson, I can attest to his guilt over having helped to develop and disseminate the progressive virus. That guilt drove him to try and walk-back his progressive dogma. I was part of a class taught by Coulson made up of third year clinical psychologists in training. Virtually of us in that class had been thoroughly exposed to the progressive virus beginning in middle school.

The resistance Coulson encountered from these soon to be doctors of clinical psychology was palpable, at times erupting into heated devaluation of Coulson, despite his illustrious career and cogent writings and lectures. It was clear to this student that had Coulson taught a class on Person-Centered Psychotherapy, peppering his lectures with stories about how he, Abraham

---

[36] Fritz Perls, "Gestalt Therapy Verbatim", 1969.

Maslow and Carl Rogers came to view the world, Coulson would have been treated like a rock-star. Instead, he was imagined by self-assured, high-esteemed selfish brats to be tantamount to a father who was scolding them for being selfish brats.

Coulson considered humanistic psychology to be fundamentally flawed because it failed to discern the true nature of man. Humanistic psychologists and their pseudo-psychologist entrepreneur brethren had failed to discern the true nature of man and what truly motivated them to become mental gurus.

This failure to deal with the true nature of man was because first, and foremost, there is no "true" as that notion has been deleted from rational discourse by the progressive virus. Furthermore, since the virus convinces man that he is the center of the universe and without him nothing else would exist, there can be no counterpoint to God that takes the form of evil. Coulson recognized the connection I'm making here:

> "But we didn't have a doctrine of evil. (Abraham) Maslow saw that we failed to understand the reality of evil in the human life. When we implied to people that they could trust their impulses, they also understood us to mean that they could

trust their evil impulses, that they weren't really evil. *But they were evil.*" [37] (Emphasis added)

Not only did Maslow, Rogers, Perls and Coulson encourage their students, clients and patients to trust and give into their impulses, but they helped to create the belief that the highest achievement in life is to indulge with abandon one's wants wishes and desires. If the patient, student or client had a functional immune system, it was soon forcibly destroyed by the progressive virus. Guilt was replaced with the adoption of hedonism.

The mechanism of action of the virus relied upon passive, non-judgmental therapy techniques and through the use of transference wherein the doctor or mental guru comes to represent the conscience of the gullible patient. Due to progressive's distortions, however, the doctor or mental guru could not function as a real conscience because he or she had been trained to forego judgment, especially moral judgment, no matter how heinous or antisocial his patient, client or student may behave. The only conscience role played by mental gurus is to brow beat their unwitting clients into artificially high self-esteem and forcing them to repeat humanistic tripe designed to

---

[37] Coulson, Charles. How I Wrecked the I. H. M.. Nuns.The Latin Mass, Chronicle of Catholic Reform, Special Edition, 1994.

ameliorate, for a time, the symptoms of a progressive infection. This is the epitome of irony.

Coulson credits Maslow for his own resilient immune system which permitted some resistance to the progressive virus that was everywhere in the 60s.

> "Maslow believed in evil, and we didn't. (referencing Rogers and Coulson) Maslow said there was danger in our thinking and acting as if there were no paranoids or psychopaths or SOBs to mess things up. We created a miniature utopian society, the encounter group." [38]

As successful as the psychologists and pseudo-psychologist entrepreneurs were at honing the progressive virus, it was left to government (public) school educators to write the remaining portions of the progressive virus and to create an epidemic of mass proportions.

---

[38] Ibid.

CHAPTER FIVE

Indoctrination on a Mass Scale

FORMALIZED INOCULATION WITH THE progressive virus began in the 1960s in universities across the country. When those college grads entered the marketplace, they brought with them their infection. They spread the infection to everyone they came in contact with. As they matured and took leadership roles in public schools and government, those same institutions became breeding grounds and indoctrination camps for the progressive virus.

Social engineering became job number one for those progressives dedicated to revolution. The handiwork of these social engineers was dedicated to creating a generation of Americans who possessed artificially high self-esteem, were self-obsessed and who were cultivated within a judgment free environment. Reading, writing and arithmetic took a back seat to the imposition of multiculturalism, amorality, lack of discipline and the promotion of self-assertion. The anxious and insecure student of the 50s was replaced with the cocky, high esteemed and self-assertive student who was no longer subordinate to the institution or his teacher and behaved more like a peer, with equal power and authority.

Entitlement became the norm among public school students. They were entitled to have their say, do their own thing, were provided a million and one excuses for their inability to write, speak and do math. They were entitled to their own mispronunciations, were entitled to dress virtually any way they so desired and were entitled to a discipline and judgment free environment. Discipline went right out the door along with traditional values. Boys and girls were homogenized and taught to disregard gender differences because those feelings were characterized as nothing but a reflection of gender oppression. Middle school children acted like adults but with none of the responsibilities.

Sexual behavior in middle school is a good indicator of the presence of the progressive virus in action. Laura Session Stepp researched the incidence of oral sex in middle school. Writing for the Washington Post in an investigative article that appeared in the summer of 1999, Ms. Stepp interviewed Michael Schaeffer, a supervisor for health education in Prince George's County, Maryland, for the past 15 years. Schaeffer told Stepp that "It (referring to oral sex) is now the expected minimum behavior." Deborah Roffman, a human sexuality consultant to 15 schools in the Baltimore-Washington corridor, was also quoted by Stepp, "I've been teaching in schools for 30 years. I am receiving an increasing number of inquiries about incidents of oral sex among young adolescents, both at parties and occasionally at school." [39]

Patricia Hersch is the author of the book *A Tribe Apart: A Journey Into the Heart of American Adolescence*. She wrote this:

> "To me, oral sex was more intimate than intercourse. Kids today absolutely don't see it that way. It's done commonly, with a shrug. It's part of the grab bag of sexual activities." [40]

Bill Ayers, writer and educator and someone who has had a profound impact on teaching teachers, described his blueprint for public education in America:

> "I began teaching when I was 20 years old in a small freedom school affiliated with the Civil Rights Movement in the United States. The year was 1965, and I'd been arrested in a demonstration. Jailed for ten days, I met several activists who were finding ways to link teaching and education with deep and fundamental social change. They were following Dewey and DuBois,

---

[39] Washington Post. By: Laura Sessions Stepp. *Unsettling new fad alarms parents:* Middle School Oral Sex. July 8, 1999.

[40] Hersch, Patricia. A Tribe Apart: A Journey into the Heart of American Adolescence. Ballantine books, 1999.

King and Helen Keller who wrote: "We can't have education without revolution. We have tried peace education for 1,900 years and it has failed. Let us try revolution and see what it will do now."[41]

Ayers is a prolific writer whose works are designed to indoctrinate and infect teachers in training with the progressive virus. It is more likely than not that your children's public school teachers have been indoctrinated with Mr. Ayer's writings.

• *Education: An American Problem.* Bill Ayers, Radical Education Project, 1968, ASIN B0007H31HU OCLC 33088998

• *Hot town: Summer in the City: I ain't gonna work on Maggie's farm no more*, Bill Ayers, Students for a Democratic Society, 1969, ASIN B000713CMI

• *Prairie Fire: The Politics of Revolutionary Anti-Imperialism*, Bernardine Dohrn, Jeff Jones, Billy Ayers, Celia Sojourn, Communications Co., 1974, ASIN B000GF2KVQ OCLC 1177495

• *The Good Preschool Teacher: Six Teachers Reflect on Their Lives*, William Ayers, Teachers College Press, 1989, ISBN 978-0-8077-2946-5

• *To Teach: The Journey of a Teacher*, William Ayers, Teachers College Press, 1993, ISBN 978-0-8077-3262-5

• *To Become a Teacher: Making a Difference in Children's Lives*, William Ayers, Teachers College Press, 1995, ISBN 978-0-8077-3455-1

• *City Kids, City Teachers: Reports from the Front Row*, William Ayers (Editor) and Patricia Ford (Editor), New Press, 1996, ISBN 978-1-56584-328-8

---

[41] Ayers, Bill.. Speech at the World Economic Forum in Caracas, Venezuela, 2006.

- *A Kind and Just Parent*, William Ayers, Beacon Press, 1997, <u>ISBN 978-0-8070-4402-5</u>
- *A Light in Dark Times: Maxine Greene and the Unfinished Conversation*, Maxine Greene (Editor), William Ayers (Editor), Janet L. Miller (Editor), Teachers College Press, 1998, <u>ISBN 978-0-8077-3721-7</u>
- *Teaching for Social Justice: A Democracy and Education Reader*, William Ayers (Editor), Jean Ann Hunt (Editor), Therese Quinn (Editor), 1998, <u>ISBN 978-1-56584-420-9</u>
- *Teacher Lore: Learning from Our Own Experience*, William H. Schubert (Editor) and William
C. Ayers (Editor), Educator's International Press, 1999, <u>ISBN 978-1-891928-03-1</u>
- *Teaching from the Inside Out: The Eight-Fold Path to Creative Teaching and Living*, Sue Sommers (Author), William Ayers (Foreword), Authority Press, 2000, <u>ISBN 978-1-929059-02-7</u>
- *A Simple Justice: The Challenge of Small Schools*, William Ayers, Teachers College Press, 2000, ISBN 978-0-8077-3963-1
- *Zero Tolerance: Resisting the Drive for Punishment*, William Ayers (Editor), Rick Ayers (Editor), Bernardine Dohrn (Editor), Jesse L. Jackson (Author), New Press, 2001, <u>ISBN 978-1-56584-666-1</u>
- *A School of Our Own: Parents, Power, and Community at the East Harlem Block Schools*, Tom Roderick (Author), William Ayers (Author), Teachers College Press, 2001, <u>ISBN 978-0-8077-4157-3</u>
- *Refusing Racism: White Allies and the Struggle for Civil Rights*, Cynthia Stokes Brown (Author), William Ayers (Editor), Therese Quinn (Editor), Teachers College Press, 2002, ISBN 978-0-8077-4204-4
- *On the Side of the Child: Summerhill Revisited*, William Ayers, Teachers College Press, 2003, ISBN 978-0-8077-4400-0

Bill Ayers must have mellowed over the years, yes? In 2001 Ayers told Chicago Magazine that he had no regrets, and urged children to "kill your parents." [42] In the same year Ayers urged children to "kill your parents," he worked as an editor, along with his wife Bernadine Dohrn, on a book written for public school teachers and administrators entitled: *Zero Tolerance: Resisting the Drive for Punishment.* One has to wonder about Ayer's motive underlying his push to remove all forms of punishment from public schools given his command to children, "kill your parents."

All of Ayer's writings are peppered with revolutionary themes. He and his wife promote the "collective" over rugged individualism and never miss an opportunity to skewer America's founding fathers. To say that Mr. Ayers and his wife despise traditional America would be an understatement. The fact that Ayers managed to infiltrate America's public schools was an act of brilliance on his part and an act of abject stupidity on the part of traditional America. Who was guarding the doors to the schoolhouse?

Ayer's attraction to the progressive virus derives from his awareness of how he can use the symptoms of a progressive virus infection to foment revolution. Likewise, Bernadine Dohrn,

---

[42] Chicago Magazine, Interview with William Ayers, 2001.

has not minced words when it comes to her real and final purpose:

> "The majority of people who are activists have stayed the course in a way, in a variety of ways. Devoted to overthrowing everything hateful about this government and corporate structure that we live in. Capitalism itself, herself...himself."[43]

Think that Ms. Dohrn has been marginalized because of her overt desire to overthrow capitalism and replace it with a socialist, Marxist system? Think again, Ms. Dohrn is a professor at Northwestern University.

Bernadine Dohrn's life has mirrored that of Simon de Beauvoir, including drug experimentation, affiliations with anarchist groups, hatred of capitalism and close identification with feminism and lesbian issues. Dohrn is an avowed anti-American revolutionary who has written books and given lectures designed to infect her audience with the progressive virus.

What should be disconcerting is that most parents have absolutely no idea that *avowed* progressive revolutionaries have infiltrated America's public school system and have been, since

---

[43] Bernadine Dohrn. Speaking to a Reunion of the Students for a Democratic Society (SDS) 2007.

the 1960s, infecting children and their teachers with their poisonous vaccine. Is it any wonder that a half-century later America is in the throes of a virulent progressive virus epidemic?

Is it mere coincidence that the provenance of the current power brokers in Washington are directly linked to Ayers, Dohrn, et al? In a well-researched and sourced article appearing in The Blaze, that provenance was outlined:

> "BERNARDINE DOHRN: She outranked her husband Ayers in the early SDS hierarchy, serving as one of 10 National Committee members and the only woman. Dohrn, Ayers and Jeff Jones created the splinter Weather Underground where an FBI informant testified the trio was willing to kill the 25 million Americans they expected to resist their planned overthrow of U.S. capitalism. Then-FBI chief J. Edgar Hoover called Dohrn "the most dangerous woman in America."
>
> Dohrn and Michelle Obama both worked at Chicago's Sidley Austin law firm in 1988. Barack Obama, Dohrn and Ayers appeared together at several community events, including one organized by Mrs. Obama in her post at the University of Chicago. Today, Dohrn, an associate

professor of law at Northwestern University and founder of its Children and Family Justice Center, supports the 150 "New SDS" chapters in U.S. high schools, colleges and universities, writing, "This is the power and the inspiration of a vast, Left umbrella network with variety and vigor." [44]

To understand Ayer's, Dohrn's and their cohort's primary motivation in promoting progressive dogma one only need to look at this introduction to a speech Ayers gave to the World Economic Forum in Caracas, Venezuela in 2006:

> "President Hugo Chavez, Vice-President Vicente Rangel, Ministers Moncada and Isturiz, invited guests, *comrades*. I'm honored and humbled to be here with you this morning. I bring greetings and support from your brothers and sisters throughout North America. Welcome to the World Education Forum! Amamos la revolucion Bolivariana!"[45] (Emphasis added)

Ayers exhibited a classic pattern of those infected with the progressive virus. When hopeful, Ayers was active in Marxist groups and espoused socialist doctrinaire. When confronted

---

[44] The Blaze: Obama's Connections to the Violent SDS: Bernardine Dohrn. May 14, 2012.

[45] Ayers, Bill.. Speech at the World Economic Forum in Caracas, Venezuela, 2006.

with the inevitable despair that comes from the progressive virus, he chose anarchy and rebellion.

As a "Weatherman," Ayers attempted to bomb his way to a Marxist revolution. His despair and embrace of anarchy lifted once he recognized that he could use the progressive virus dogma to effectuate the revolution if he were only patient and infiltrated government institutions. He chose public education to practice his craft. Because of the progressive virus, public education was like a bank vault with no door and no guard. Ayers and his fellow comrades walked right in and changed public education's DNA. Ayers targeted teachers and became a very successful purveyor of and user of the progressive virus.

In April of 2012 Ayers spoke to the Occupy Wall Street Crowd in Chicago, Illinois. Ayers took questions from the crowd. One person asked him how he deals with criticism, here is what he said:

> "I get up every morning thinking, today I'm gonna make a difference. Today I'm gonna end capitalism. Today I'm gonna make a revolution. I go to bed every night disappointed, but I'm back again tomorrow. That's the only way you can do it." [46]

---

[46] Bill Ayers. Speaking to members of Occupy Wall Street in Chicago, Illinois. April 1, 2012.

The clinical transformation of the 60s generation into the progressives we see today is seemingly stunning. The 60s generation rebelled against any authority, and especially against anyone imposing their will upon them. They transformed into intolerant and tyrannical martinets who are intent upon forcing their will on their fellow citizens.

Such a transformation is only stunning if one fails to comprehend what the 60s revolutionaries were all about. The 60s crowd was comprised of the same nascent tyrannical progressives we see today, but their behavior was shrouded within the cloaking garb of "peace, love and long hair." Hippies were passive-aggressive, but they were still aggressive. Their rebellion and self-indulgence was tempered and not fully realized because the progressive virus had not yet overwhelmed their native culture. Once it had, they became who they always were: Self-obsessed narcissists intent upon having things their way.

CHAPTER SIX

The Sickness Takes Hold

IN DECEMBER OF 2011 The Pew Research Center published a survey that found:

> "46% of Americans hold a disapproving view that rich people are wealthy because they were fortunate enough to be born into money or have the right connections. But almost as many people — 43% — say wealthy people are rich "mainly because of their own hard work, ambition or education." [47]

In early 2012 professor of economics Jack Chambless had his students at Valencia College, located in Orlando, Florida, write an essay on the role of government in their lives. Chambless reported the results of his study, the results of which illustrate the success that the likes of Bill Ayers and his wife have had on America's students:

---

[47] Pew based its findings on interviews with 2,048 adults by cell phone or landline from Dec. 6-19, 2011. The poll has a margin of error of plus or minus 2.9 percentage points for all respondents, higher for subgroups.

"I took the essays from three classes – about 180 students. About 10% of the students said they wanted the government to leave them alone and not tax them too much and let them regulate their own lives. But over 80% of the students said that the American dream to them meant a job, a house, and plenty of money for retirement and vacations and things like this. When it came to the part about the federal government, eight out of ten students said they wanted free health care, they wanted the government to pay for their tuition, they wanted the government to pay for the down payment on their house, they expected the government to, quote, "give them a job." Many of them said they wanted the government to tax wealthier individuals so that they would have an opportunity to have a better life.

What follows is a representative essay written by one of professor Chambless's students:

"As human beings, we are not really responsible for our own acts, and so we need government to control those who don't care about others."

These data suggest that traditional values are holding on by a thread in the face of a widespread progressive epidemic.

On February 23, 2012, a Georgetown Law student by the name of Sandra Fluke testified as the lone witness in a House of Representatives, unofficial Democratic-sponsored hearing. While the rest of the Capitol was mostly empty, Democratic leader Nancy Pelosi, three other Democrats and dozens of mainly young women supporters crowded into a House office building room to applaud Fluke as she spoke of the importance of reproductive health care to women.

Fluke's comments represent the end result of her progressive-infected education.

> "[W]ithout insurance coverage, contraception can cost a woman over $3,000 during law school. For a lot of students who, like me, are on public interest scholarships, that's practically an entire summer's salary. Forty percent of female students at Georgetown Law report struggling financially as a result of this policy. One told us of how embarrassed and powerless she felt when she was standing at the pharmacy counter, learning for the first time that contraception wasn't covered, and had to walk away because

she couldn't afford it. Women like her have no choice but to go without contraception." [48]

I'm going to put aside, for arguments sake, the cost of birth control pills, estimated to cost between $15 and $50 per month. This translates into a cost, over three years, of $540 to $1,800, not the $3,000 dollars quoted by Ms. Fluke. Some sellers, e.g. Wall-Mart, sell oral contraceptives for around $10 dollars a month. Regardless, it is Sandra Fluke's attitude, not her shopping and math skills, that is worthy of discussion. [49]

Fluke essentially demanded that her fellow citizens, either directly or indirectly, pay for costs associated with her discretionary sexual activities. Not mentioned, but certainly implied, is that if one cost of her elective sexual behavior is the prevention of pregnancy in the form of oral contraceptives, then the increased need to screen for STDs would also be included in the costs she demanded be paid for by someone other than she. Fluke knew that when she enrolled in Georgetown Law School that it was a Jesuit institution and that Georgetown's insurance did not cover birth control pills and devices.

Fluke spoke with surety as she expressed her sense of entitlement. If the pleasure that comes from engaging in

---

[48] House of Representative, Special Hearing on Reproductive Rights. February 23, 2012.

[49] Planned Parenthood: *Birth Control Pills at a Glance.*
http://www.plannedparenthood.org/health-topics/birth-control/birth-control-pill-4228.htm.

recreational sex was competing with Fluke's personal responsibility to the child she may create, it would be a foregone conclusion that Fluke would not only choose her own pleasure and freedom to do whatever she wants, but that she also believes that she is *entitled* to have someone else pick up the cost. Ms. Fluke made it crystal clear that she was *entitled to demand, in fact expect*, that a Catholic institution and its insurance carrier subordinate its principles to suit her wants. She came to Congress, at Ms. Pelosi's request, to engage in a staged drama that was intended to coerce and force a Catholic institution and its insurance carrier to bend to the will of government.

Rogers, Maslow, Perls and the pseudo-psychologist entrepreneurs should rejoice at having helped to create Fluke's sense of entitlement. No one dared during the hearing to bring up the subject of personal responsibility. Fluke was surrounded by politicians who, like she, had been consumed by the progressive virus. The informal House hearing was judgment, values and guilt free. It was progressive drama at its best.

The progressive virus mandates, after all, that the most important thing in life is to indulge wants, wishes and desires, feel good above all else and displace responsibility for errors, omissions and shortcomings (if there are such things), to other people or an unjust society. To say otherwise, is immediately attacked by the virus that declares that there is no right and wrong, only oppression as manifest by social injustice. And that oppression is defined in part, as it was by Ms. Fluke, as anyone who would dare suggest that if she desires to sexually recreate, then she or her family, not someone else, should pay for it.

As one might expect, conservative commentators attacked Ms. Fluke, using any number of pejorative and tasteless adjectives. In response, none other than the President of the United States, Barack Obama, phoned Ms. Fluke to ostensibly both console and praise her for her testimony. By his act, President Obama reinforced Ms. Fluke's sense of entitlement and reinforced her belief that a Jesuit institution, through its insurance carrier, had an obligation to pay for her discretionary sexual behavior, an obligation the president intended to enforce, using the coercive power of the United States government.

Ms. Fluke exhibited florid proof of her sense of entitlement, assuredness and the displacement of responsibility during her testimony. Her testimony was characterized by an abject absence of guilt, angst or humility. But what else would we expect, given that Ms. Fluke was a shining example of American education. In his book *Freefall of the American University*, James Nelson Black wrote this:

"[A]las, this is where we find the universities today, populated to a surprising degree by a generation of bourgeois ideologists schooled in the faddish Marxism of the sixties. These men and women, who cut themselves adrift from the common culture and traditional beliefs, have taken the reins of power in the schools and are now laboring to transform the basic structures of society from the bottom up. In this, I'm reminded of the often-quoted boast of Norman Thomas, a Princeton-educated Presbyterian minister and a founding member of the ACLU who was defeated six times in his bid for the White House on the Socialist Party ticket. In 1952, no doubt, his words provoked only laughter, but today they offer a more somber warning. Thomas had once said in a candid interview that, *"The American people will never knowingly adopt socialism, but under the name of liberalism they will adopt every fragment of the socialist program until one day America will be a socialist nation without ever knowing how it happened."* By 1970, both Thomas and Gus Hall, the perennial candidate of the Communist Party USA, gave up their quest for the presidency because, as they said, the two major parties had already adopted their platforms. But their legacy is with us still." [50]

(Emphasis added)

Should there be any functional remnants of Locke's and de Tocqueville's ideas residing in dorms and classrooms, the progressive virus eradicates them with cruel and ruthless efficiency as soon as they are voiced.

In 2003 Anne Neal testified before a Senate Committee on Health, Education, Labor and Pensions. The Senate committee was formed to look into the lack of intellectual diversity within American universities.

Neal testified in her capacity as president of the American Council of Trustees and Alumni. Neal spoke about the problems of disinviting controversial speakers, the punishment of faculty members who fail to conform to the dominant progressive ideology, and the predominance of one-sided courses and opinions among the faculty. Virtually with no exception, those courses and opinions were designed to promote and infect as many students as possible with the progressive virus.

Neal testified that students who resist being infected with the progressive virus live in daily fear of reprisal or caricature if

---

[50] Black, James Nelson. Freefall of the AMERICAN UNIVERSITY. How Our Colleges Are CORRUPTING THE MINDS AND MORALS of the Next Generation.

they speak their minds, and they are routinely victimized by draconian speech codes and ideological litmus tests that place unfair restraints on their constitutional guarantee of free speech. [51]

Given public education's emphasis upon social engineering, has academic achievement been compromised? In 2011 CNN contributor William J. Bennet filed this report:

> "Last week, the College Board dealt parents, teachers and the education world a serious blow. According to its latest test results, "SAT reading scores for the high school class of 2011 were the lowest on record, and combined reading and math scores fell to their lowest point since 1995." [52]

In Illinois, the home state of the current President of the United States, like virtually everywhere else in America, students simply don't make grades like they used to.

> "About half of Illinois public high school students flunked state exams in reading, math and science this year, the worst performance in the history of

---

[51] Senate Hearing on Health, Education, Labor and Pensions. Anne Neal, Witness, 2003.

[52] CNN. William Bennett, Contributor. Record Low SAT Scores a Wake Up Call. September 21, .2011.

the 11th grade Prairie State Achievement Examination, statewide test results show." [53]

Test scores from cities and states across the United States are similar to these data. When it comes to assessing how American children perform when compared to the rest of the industrial world, it becomes clear that something is terribly wrong with our public schools:

- American students rank 25th in math and 21st in science compared to students in 30 industrialized countries.
- America's top math students rank 25th out of 30 countries when compared with top students elsewhere in the world.
- By the end of 8th grade, U.S. students are two years behind in the math being studied by peers in other countries.
- Sixty eight percent of 8th graders can't read proficiently, and most will never catch up.
- More than 1.2 million students drop out of school every year. That's more than 6,000 students every school day and one every 26 seconds.
- The national high school graduation rate is only 70 percent, with states ranging from a high of 84 percent in Utah to a low of 54 percent in South Carolina.
- Graduation rates are much lower for minority students. Only about half of the nation's African-American and Latino students graduate on time from high school.
- The poverty rate for families headed by dropouts is more than twice that of families headed by high school graduates.
- Nearly 44 percent of dropouts under age 24 are jobless, and the unemployment rate of high school dropouts older than 25 is more than three times that of college graduates.

---

[53] Chicago Tribune. By Diane Rado and Tara Malone, Tribune reporters. October 20, 2011.

- Over a lifetime, dropouts earn $260,000 less than high school graduates.
- The health of an 18-year-old high school dropout is similar to that of a more educated person over two decades older.
- Dropouts from the class of 2007 will cost our nation more than $300 billion in lost wages, lost taxes and lost productivity.
- Dropouts contribute about $60,000 less in federal and state income taxes. Each cohort of dropouts costs the U.S. $192 billion in lost income and taxes.
- Sixty five percent of U.S. convicts are dropouts and lack of education is one of the strongest predictors of criminal activity.
- A dropout is more than eight times as likely to be in jail or prison as a high school graduate and nearly 20 times as likely as a college graduate.
- For each additional year of schooling, the odds that a student will someday commit a crime like murder or assault are reduced by almost one-third.
- Each year, the U.S. spends $9,644 per student compared to $22,600 per prison inmate.
- Increasing the high school completion rate by just one percent for all men ages 20 to 60 would save the U.S. up to $1.4 billion per year in reduced costs from crime. [54]

Not only are public school students poorly prepared, their ethics suggests that the progressive virus has changed the very character of American public school students. Take a look at these statistics:

- 80% of "high-achieving" high school students admit to cheating.

---

[54] The Broad Foundation. Educational Statistics, 2007.

- 51% of high school students did not believe cheating was wrong.
- 95% of cheating high school students said that they had not been detected.
- 75% of college students admitted cheating, and 90% of college students didn't believe cheaters would be caught.
- Almost 85% of college students said cheating was necessary to get ahead. [55]

Professor Donald McCabe, a leading expert in academic integrity, conducted a study of over 4500 high school students in May of 2001. Here is what professor McCabe found:

- 72% of students reported one or more instances of serious cheating on written work
- 15% had submitted a paper obtained in large part from a term paper mill or website
- 52% had copied a few sentences from a website w/o citing the source
- over 45% admitted to collaborating inappropriately with others on assignments. [56]

In a sample of 1,800 students at nine state universities:

- 70% of the students admitted to cheating on exams
- 84% admitted to cheating on written assignments
- 52% had copied a few sentences from a website w/o citing the source. [57]

---

[55] U.S. News and World Report, November 22, 1999.
[56] McCabe, Donald L. and Linda Klebe Trevino. "Academic Dishonesty: Honor Codes and Other Contextual Influences." Journal of Higher Education 64.5 (Sep.-Oct. 1993): 522-38.
[57] McCabe, D. L., & Trevino, L. K. (1996). "What we know about cheating in college: Longitudinal trends and recent developments." Change, 28(1), 28-33. (EJ 520 088)

In 2002, in a study that screened 4,500 high school students, it was found that 75 percent of them engage in serious cheating.

> "[M]ore than half have plagiarized work they found on the Internet. Perhaps most disturbing, many of them don't see anything wrong with cheating: Some 50 percent of those responding to the survey said they don't consider copying questions and answers from a test is even cheating." [58]

Students are entering colleges and universities with experience in cheating and rationales for committing this act. A survey on academic integrity at the college level included comments from college students that capture the impact progressive thought has on cheating:

- "I actually think cheating is good. A person who has an entirely honest life can't succeed these days."
- "We students know that the fact is we are almost completely judged on our grades. They are so important that we will sacrifice our own integrity to make a good impression." [59]

Here us what the Educational Testing Service has to say about cheating:

---

[58] Rutger's Management Education Center, National Survey of Academic Integrity, 2002.
[59] Ibid.

- Statistics show that cheating among high school students has risen dramatically during the past 50 years.
- In the past it was the struggling student who was more likely to cheat just to get by. Today it is also the above-average college bound students who are cheating.
- 73% of all test takers, including prospective graduate students and teachers agree that most students do cheat at some point. 86% of high school students agreed.
- Cheating no longer carries the stigma that it used to. Less social disapproval coupled with increased competition for admission into universities and graduate schools has made students more willing to do whatever it takes to get the A.
- Grades, rather than education, have become the major focus of many students.
- Fewer college officials (35%) believe that cheating is a problem in this country than do members of the public (41%).
- High school students are less likely than younger test takers to report cheaters, because it would be "tattling" or "ratting out a friend."
- Many students feel that their individual honesty in academic endeavors will not affect anyone else.
- While about 20% of college students admitted to cheating in high school during the 1940s, today between 75 and 98 percent of college students surveyed each year report having cheated in high school.
- Students who cheat often feel justified in what they are doing. They cheat because they see others cheat and they think they will be unfairly disadvantaged. The cheaters are getting 100 on the exam, while the non-cheaters may only get 90s.
- In most cases cheaters don't get caught. If caught, they seldom are punished severely, if at all.
- Cheating increases due to pressure for high grades.

- Math and Science are the courses in which cheating most often occurs.
- Computers can make cheating easier than ever before. For example, students can download term papers from the World Wide Web.
- "Thirty years ago, males admitted to significantly more academic dishonesty than females. Today, that difference has decreased substantially and some recent studies show no differences in cheating between men and women in college."
- Cheating may begin in elementary school when children break or bend the rules to win competitive games against classmates. It peaks during high school when about 75% of students admit to some sort of academic misgivings.
- Research about cheating among elementary age children has shown that: There are more opportunities and motivations to cheat than in preschool; Young children believe that it is wrong, but could be acceptable depending on the task; Do not believe that it is common; Hard to resist when others suggest breaking rules; Need for approval is related to cheating; Boys cheat more.
- Academic cheating begins to set in at the junior high level.
- Research about cheating among middle school children (Ages 12-14) has shown that: There is increased motivation to cheat because there is more emphasis on grades; Even those students who say it is wrong, cheat; If the goal is to get a good grade, they will cheat.
- According to one recent survey of middle schoolers, 2/3 of respondents reported cheating on exams, while 9/10 reported copying another's homework.
- According to the 1998 poll of Who's Who Among American High School Students, 80% of the country's best students cheated to get to the top of their class. More than half the students surveyed said they don't think cheating is a big deal – and most did not get caught.

- According to surveys conducted by The Josephson Institute of Ethics among 20,000 middle and high school students, 64% of high school students admitted to cheating in 1996. That number jumped to 70% in 1998.

- Research about cheating among college students has shown the following to be the primary reasons for cheating: Campus norm; No honor code; Penalties not severe; Faculty support of academic integrity policies is low; Little chance of being caught; Incidence is higher at larger, less selective institutions.

- Additional influencers include: Others doing it; Faculty member doesn't seem to care; Required course; No stated rules or rules are unclear; Heavy workload.

- Profile of college students more likely to cheat: Business or Engineering majors; Those whose future plans include business; Men self-report cheating more than woman; Fraternity and Sorority members; Younger students; Students with lower GPAs or those at the very top.

- Cheating is seen by many students as a means to a profitable end.

- Cheating does not end at graduation. For example, resume fraud is a serious issue for employers concerned about the level of integrity of new employees. "[60]

---

[60] Educational Testing Service. www.nocheating.org. 2011.

CHAPTER SEVEN

The Millennials

YOUNG AMERICANS JUST ENTERING the work force represent the end result of over a quarter-century of progressive indoctrination. These young men and women number approximately 80 million. They were born between 1980 and 1995. Millennials were raised to believe that they were all stars in the making.

Competition was tempered or non-existent for Millennials. They played in little league baseball where there were no winners or losers and everyone got a trophy at the end of the season. Girls and boys were homogenized to the point where any differences were presumed to be purely psychological, not biological. It is a generation that found some parents raising their children as gender neutral, that is, no his or hers, pink or blue, trucks or dolls, dresses or pants, short or long hair.

Sexuality is viewed as pleasure with no responsibility. School teachers find it perfectly normal to act like the children they are teaching. Long gone are the students who feel insecure or lack self-esteem or self-assertion skills. Millennials have been, since they were old enough to talk, treated as though their opinions on complex issues of life, death, economics and values are just as valuable and meaningful as a 50 year-old war veteran with a family who is signing the checks that pay for their lifestyle.

Millennials have lived in a self-indulgent world where the only discipline they received, if you can call it discipline, was a "time out" from their digital devices when they failed to perform. They are, for the most part, adrift in a sea of non-attachment, save for their "friends" on Facebook or other social media. They not only have no allegiance to their country, they are more likely to blame America first for any perceived inequity in outcomes. Religion is likely to be perceived as myth and in its place we find a blind adherence to the religion of the environment and pure adoration for self.

The harsh reality is that despite having been indoctrinated in progressive dogma, and despite laboring under the belief that they define reality, the objective realities of life are beginning to challenge Millennials who were poisoned by the progressive virus.

The Wechsler Adult Intelligence Scale is a deviation intelligence test that was originally developed in the 1930s and updated over 80 years since then to remove any cultural bias. It is considered to be a premier, culture free measure of intelligence. When compared to non-verbal intelligence tests (cultural free by definition), e.g., Raven Progressive Matrices

Test, Naglieri Nonverbal Abilities Test and the Universal Nonverbal Intelligence Test, the statistical distribution of intelligence scores on the Wechsler is remarkably similar.

The distribution of intelligence scores among the population at large approximates a normal distribution. This distribution includes Millennials. Using the Wechsler test as an example, 68% of the millions of adults and children who have been tested fall within the range of 90 to 109. Statistically we know that the vast majority of people are of average intelligence. In practice terms this means that they can perform average tasks of reasoning and information processing at a normal level. These people are not going to be neurosurgeons, brilliant physicists or other professions that require a much higher level of horsepower, i.e., intelligence.

Average people are the norm. Normal people have difficulty understanding metaphors, e.g., What does this saying mean? *Shallow brooks are noisy.* Having administered the Wechsler over a thousand times to people from all walks of life, average intelligence people tend to answer that question using literal and concrete reasoning, e.g., "Well, if the water is shallow it is likely to make more noise."

Comedian and social commentator Chris Rock says this in his standup routine, and I paraphrase. "If you go into any classroom in the country, you find two really smart kids, two really dumb kids and the rest are average." He had it about right.

Looking closer at the distribution of intelligence, approximately 84% of all people possess average or *lower* intelligence. As intelligence diminishes, perception, reasoning, with particular reference to abstract reasoning using words and concepts dramatically decreases.

High performers in intelligence-intensive professions often possess intelligence scores that represent the top 1 or 2 percent or so of all people on earth. Thomas J. Bouchard, Jr. and Nancy L. Segal published research consistent with a voluminous data set accumulated over the years that proves that approximately 70% of the variance in intelligence scores of identical twins was found to be associated with genetic variation. Consistent with other research, monozygotic twins (identical genetics) reared apart were eerily similar to identical twins reared together on various measures of personality, occupational and leisure-time interests, and social attitudes. [61]

To be clear, heritability is not the equivalence of inevitability. What is clear is that people inherit a ceiling when it comes to intelligence. They also inherit special talent that is rare, by definition, such as a special musical ability (The late Whitney

---

[61] Bouchard TJ Jr, Lykken DT, McGue M, Segal NL, Tellegen A (1990). "Sources of human psychological differences: the Minnesota Study of Twins Reared Apart". Science 250 (4978): 223–228.

Houston's God-given voice, Yo-Yo Ma's ability to play the cello); visuomotor skills as demonstrated by pitching star Nolan Ryan, the late baseball pitcher Satchel Paige or basketball star Michael Jordan or the late heart surgeon Michael Debakey, M.D. These people were born gifted and represent the top 1% of God-given ability.

Hard work plus special talent and a little luck equals greatness, hard work absent special talent equals a different kind of success, no less noble than the hard work plus special talent version, but certainly if you are a Millennial, you expect greatness, not merely success. In fact, you are convinced that you deserve and are entitled to it. But as with all lies, sooner or later the truth has a way of creeping into one's brainwashed fantasies.

Millennials were raised to believe that they are all nascent executives, surgeons, brilliant ball players, leaders and captains of industry (think of Alex Rodriguez, Ronald Reagan or Steve Jobs). To maintain this illusion, Millennial children have been shielded from the forces of natural selection. As we have already noted, they played games with no winner or loser, their teachers routinely gave them "stars" and all of them were awarded performance trophies regardless of their performance. Tens of thousands of Millennials were subjected to "Baby Einstein"[62] while they were still in their cribs. Notice the name: "Baby *Einstein*, not "Baby Smart" or "Baby Exceptional." Millennials were raised by progressive infested parents who took literally the notion of the tabula raza.

Millennials have never been subjected to the natural selection forces of a pickup basketball game where the best players are chosen first. On the other hand, they have been "hot housed" to a degree never seen before in America. Millennials have been tutored, coached, mentored, propped up and, in some instances, "taught to the test", so that they could score well on standardized achievement tests.

Millennials are like the child who puts a towel around his neck and jumps into the air like Superman, but instead of falling and learning a lesson, his progressive infected parent sneaks up on her child and lifts him. The doting parent "flys" her child around the living room until he shows a desire to land, at which point the parent puts him

---

[62] "We thought that families deserved better," said Dr. Alvin F. Poussaint, a psychiatrist at Judge Baker Children's Center and member of the CCFC Steering Committee. "Marketing of baby videos plays to parents' natural tendency to want what is best for their children. We believe that in response to our advocacy, Disney is now offering a full refund to parents who bought Baby Einstein videos." The American Academy of Pediatrics recommends no screen time for children under the age of two.

down gently and slips away leaving the child with the belief that he *is* Superman.

Since virtually every Millennial child was brainwashed to believe that exposed to the right environment he or she can be brilliant at math, know how to spell intuitively, be a brilliant pianist, run fast, catch a ball behind his back and a never ending series of similar lies, disappointment was inevitable. Reality raises its ugly head sooner or later.

When the budding Millennial geniuses were forced to grapple with the reality that some kids run faster, are smarter, better looking and have more energy, the specter of failure wraps itself around the Millennial like a bad odor you can't get rid of no matter what you do. But never fear, the Millennials have built in excuses for their average performance.

Progressives, as part of their brainwashing of Millennials, included promoting in them an exaggerated version of the defense mechanism of displacement. The ease with which Millennials blame society, cultural deficits, their parents, the world, capitalists, their teachers, their lot in life, ad infinitum, is striking. Seldom can the Millennial acknowledge that underneath all the coaching, mentoring and tutoring he or she is probably average and is discontent because of the progressive brainwashing to which they have been subjected. When they run out of excuses for their performance deficits, they tune out and focus their energy on their social networks and leisure activities. They skip from job to job like a patron sampling selections at a Sunday buffet. They cannot tolerate constructive criticism, and if you are an employer, you have to be part psychoanalyst and doting parent if you want to keep your Millennial employee around to do work. In 2008 CBS *60 Minutes* explored the phenomenon of the Millennial generation.

Morley Safer: [J]ust take me through some of the do's and dont's on how you must speak to this generation of young workers.

Marion Saltzman [63]: You do have to speak to them a little bit like a therapist on television might speak to a patient. You can't be harsh you cannot tell them you're disappointed in them. You can't really ask them to live and breathe the company because they are living and breathing themselves and that keeps them very busy.

Morley Safer: Faced with new employees who want to roll into work with their iPods and flip-flops around noon but still be CEO by Friday, companies are realizing that the button-down exec happy to have a job is as dead as the three-martini lunch.

---

[63] Marion Saltzman is an ad agency executive who has been managing and tracking Millennials since they entered the work force.

Marion Saltzman: They'll tell you what time their yoga class is and the day's work will be organized around the fact that they have this commitment.

Mary Crane [64]: [T]hey have climbed Mount Everest, they've been down to Machu Picchu to help excavate it but they've never punched a time clock. They have no idea what it's like to actually be in an office at nine-o'clock.

Morley Safer: Crane maintains that while this generation has extraordinary technical skills, childhoods filled with trophies and adulation didn't prepare them for the cold realities of work.

Marion Crane: You now have a generation coming into the workplace that has grown up with the expectation that they will automatically win and they'll always be rewarded, even for just showing up.

Morley Safer: So who's to blame for the narcissistic praise hounds now taking over the office? Wall Street Journal columnist Jeffrey Zaslow covers trends in the workplace and points the finger at the man who was once America's favorite next-door neighbor.

Jeffrey Zaslow: A guy like Mister Rogers, Fred Rogers on TV, and he was telling his pre-schoolers you're special, you're special, he meant well but we as parents ran with it, and we said, you know,

---

[64] Mary Crane is a former White House employee and teacher of Millennials.

you Jr. you're special and you're special and you're special and for doing what? We really didn't explain that.

Morley Safer: Zaslow says that the coddling virus continues to eat away even when Jr. goes off to college.

Jeffrey Zaslow: I've heard from several professors who've said, a student will come up after class and say "I don't like my grade, and my mom wants to talk to you, here's the phone." And the student thinks it's like a service, I deserve it cause I'm paying for it, what are you doing giving me a "C"?

Morley Safer: Today more than half of all college seniors move home after graduation. It's a safety net or safety diaper that allows many kids to quickly opt out of a job they don't like. There once was, if not shame, a little uneasiness about being seen to be living at home in your mid-20s.

Marion Crane: Not only is there no shame with it, but this is thought to be a very smart, wise economic decision.

Morley Safer: And dear-old mom isn't just your landlord, she's your agent as well.

Marion Crane: Career services departments are complaining about the parents who are coming to update their child's resume. And in fact if you go to employers, and they're starting to express concerns now with the parents who will phone HR and say "but my little Susie or little Johnny didn't get the performance evaluation I think they deserve.

Jason Dorsey: Our parents really took from us that opportunity to fall down on our face and learn how to stand up.

Morley Safer: Jason Dorsey and Ryan Healy both make a living advising their fellow 20-somethings on how to cope with work. Ryan started a website with that purpose and Jason has written two how-to books for them. And while he admits his mother picked out his suit for this interview, his generation is not going to make the same mistakes their parents made.

Jason Dorsey: We're not going to settle, because we saw our parents settle and we have options, that we can keep hopping jobs. No longer is it bad to have four jobs on your resume in a year, whereas for our parents or even Gen-X that was terrible...we definitely put lifestyle and friends above work, no question about it...

Morley Safer: Where does this fantasy about, I'm gonna find a dream job come from? There's no such thing as a dream job...I mean a few of us, like me, where does this fantasy come from?

Jason Dorsey: I think we were told when we were little you can be anything you want, and they went on and on...

Morley Safer: A big lie, right?...

Jason Dorsey: Big goals are great, so when your fantasy that everything is gonna be perfect and peachy is not. [65]

---

[65] CBS News 60 Minutes, with Morley Safer. *The Age of the Millennials.* May, 2008.

Reflecting back on our opening chapter that traced the roots of the progressive virus, it is clear that the provenance of the Millennial generation can be traced right back to Descartes, Sartre and their ilk who gave the progressive virus its first foothold.

The Millennials are the end result of the progressive virus having infected every American generation since the 1960s. As you can tell from the *60 Minutes* expose on Millennials, some of them have a glimmer of insight into how they got to be the way they are, but few, if any, understand that they are the handiwork of progressive revolutionaries who began as anarchists in the 60s and then graduated to infiltrating the very DNA of America.

It is concerning that most Millennials have no awareness that their generation is the product of the 60s revolutionaries who grew up to brainwash them. Their handiwork was not, for the most part, well intentioned, but a specific plan executed against the Millennials in order to foment their revolutionary goals. When Bill Ayers told children to "kill your parents," he was expressing his intent to foment revolution by breaking the bond between parents and children, and ultimately destroying the nuclear family. Once the family was destroyed, the void left behind could be filled with government and secular humanist tripe. What really occurred is that progressive parents immuno-compromised their children by infecting them with lies.

For every Millennial there exists an analog young person in Asia, The Middle East and other cultures and areas of the world not infested with the progressive virus. Those foreign-born young men and women perform better academically than their Millennial counterparts and have a work ethic that more closely resembles America in the 1940s and 50s.

One thing is for certain, for every Millennial climbing Killimanjaro or trekking his or her way across Europe, every Millennial skipping from job to job while texting their social network friends, someone is signing the check, and it isn't them. As progressivism flourishes, the check signers of the future are not going to be limited to the parents of the Millennials, but the American taxpayer.

CHAPTER EIGHT

The Progressive Virus Genome

AS WE HAVE CHRONICLED throughout this book, the progressive virus didn't take form overnight. It developed, over the millennia, in incremental steps, often times going unnoticed except during periods of viral epidemics. When these epidemics did occur, they were characterized as "cultural revolutions" as opposed to what they really were; viral infection epidemics that resulted in revolution.

Each segment of the progressive virus disrupts or destroys man's ability to perceive reality and to process information so that it comports with reality. You can see right away that one of the disruptions caused by the progressive virus is that it destroys the fact of an objective reality. The progressive virus distorts perception so that man comes to believe that he defines reality. It gets even worse, however, when defining reality the progressive virus hierarchically reshuffles all of the competing forces in the world and moves primal wants, wishes and desires to the front of the line.

What follows is a descriptive analysis of each segment of the progressive virus, cataloging it by the distortion it creates in man's cognitive function.

- **There is no Good and Bad**

  The virus convinces the mind, against common sense and practice, that all things are, what they are, because of how human beings define them. In other words, our point of view defines everything. Nothing has an inherent, objective quality. "Good" and "bad" are merely expressions of man's point of view at any given time.

- **Man is God**

  Absent an objective reality, man catapults himself into the role of God. The progressive virus forces its victim to see the world as an ever-changing terrain where nothing is inherently better than anything else. Man becomes convinced of his absolute power to define everything when infected with the virus.

- **The Ability to Discriminate is Destroyed**

  In the absence of an objective reality, everything becomes the same in terms of good or bad, right or wrong, positive or negative, virtuous or non-virtuous. The assertion that there is a difference is defined as an expression of oppression.

- **Displacement of Responsibility from Self to the Environment**

  Personal responsibility is negated and in its place is the belief that all acts and outcomes are the result of extrinsic factors. Differing outcomes means social injustice.

- **The Void Created by the Abolition of God is Filled**

  Those infected with the progressive virus fill the void left by the destruction of God with God-like worshiping of the environment, nutritional supplements and/or organic foods, mind altering substances and a libertine lifestyle or revolutionary political movements.

- **Convenient Equilibrium**

  Victims of the progressive virus feel compelled to declare balance, equilibrium or sameness when it is suggested that two or more cultures or behaviors or virtually anything are inherently distinct and/or different.

- **The Infected Impose Their Will**

  The progressive virus compels that the virus be spread and adopted. Forced infection with and adoption of the virus is effectuated through the coercive exercise of governmental power or strict enforcement of political correctness.

- **The End Justifies the Means**

  Victims of the progressive virus care little about the means by which they achieve social justice. Anything goes as long as it achieves the goal of spreading the progressive infection.

- **Mandated Multiculturalism**

  The United States was founded by Anglo-Europeans who were, for the most part, theists. These men ascribed to John Locke's and Baron de Montesquieu's, among others, anti-progressive beliefs. As a result of recognizing the threat theists represent, the progressive virus mandates that its victims nullify Anglo-European cultural beliefs. This is accomplished by systematically diminishing or eliminating Anglo-European customs and practices, including holidays, food, music, dating and marriage-customs. Anglo-European culture is ridiculed, criticized, made fun of and described as oppressive. Being an Anglo-European makes one an acceptable target for ridicule, prejudice and hatred.

- **Totalitarianism**

  Progressives feel a compulsion to control their fellow citizens. They gain control using totalitarian methods often shrouded in environmental or politically correct causes. Progressives gain control in incremental steps until one day their control is absolute.

- **Political Correctness**

Victims of the progressive virus created the "politically correct" movement. The name, "politically correct," is a misnomer in that it should be named more accurately as "progressive correct." The progressive virus is vulnerable to certain truths, voiced as truth. Therefore, the virus protects itself using pre-emptive strikes against any language rooted in truth. Violate the law and you may lose your job, be ostracized or become a social pariah.

- **The Zero Sum Economic Theory**

Those infected with the progressive virus proselytize the lynch pin to their social justice paradigm. That lynch pin is that in any economy there exists a finite sum of wealth, and when one person or group possesses any given percentage of that wealth, then the remaining members of that group have had their wealth depleted in an equal amount. In other words, if a pie has only 10 pieces and one group has six pieces, then one piece has been taken from the other group. The truth of the matter is that economies are not linear nor are they fixed. Inventions, creativity and entrepreneurship "grow the pie" and thus make more wealth available for the industrious.

Progressives are predisposed to be passive-aggressive. This makes them vulnerable or predisposed to succumb to a progressive infection. The difference between Auguste Comte and John Locke, for example, is one of personality in the first instance. If one looks closely at the behavior of the early writers of the progressive virus who succumbed to the virus, e.g., Comte, Beauvoir, Nietzsche, et al., we find a personality type vulnerable to the progressive virus. The following personality characteristics provide the virus a warm and inviting Petri dish within which to multiply.

- Dissatisfied people who behaved as though they were perpetually wounded. [66]
- Fussy people with sour and unpleasant dispositions. [67]
- Depressives with ill tempers who were spiteful, malicious, and pessimistic. [68]
- People with irritable moods. [69]
- People who took everything hard and felt the unpleasantness in every situation. [70] [71]

---

[66] Aschaffenburg, Gustav. *Crime and its Repression.* Boston. Little Brown and Company, 1913.

[67] Hellpach, Willy. Amphithymia. Zeitschrift fuer die Gestant Neurologicie und Psychiatrie 1920.

[68] Schneider, Kurt "Zeitschrift für die gesante". Neurol Psychiatry. 1920, 59: 281–86.

[69] Bleuler E. Textbook of Psychiatry. New York, The Macmillan Company, 1924.

[70] Krapelin, E. Dementia praecox and paraphrenia. (trans. Barclay, RM) Edinburgh: E.S. Livingstone. 1913/1919.

More recent scientific descriptions of passive-aggressive people include these characteristics:

- Passive resistance to fulfilling social and occupational tasks through procrastination and inefficiency;
- Complaints of being misunderstood, unappreciated, and victimized by others;
- Sullenness, irritability, and argumentativeness in response to expectations;
- Angry and pessimistic attitudes toward a variety of events;
- Unreasonable criticism and scorn toward those in authority;
- Envy and resentment toward those who are more fortunate;
- Self-definition as luckless in life and an inclination to whine and grumble about being jinxed;
- Alternating behavior between hostile assertion of personal autonomy and dependent contrition. [72]

The deep uneasiness and displeasure felt by those vulnerable to the progressive virus sets the stage for their infection with the virus. Add willfulness to this personality profile and you have a recipe for a progressive revolutionary.

Absent blaming outside events for their existential misery, and absent a dedicated effort to foment revolution, progressives spiral into a deep despair, hence their fascination with drugs and suicide.

The psychodynamic at work is this: Those vulnerable to the progressive virus feel uneasiness and unhappiness *before* they

---

[71] Millon, T. & Radovanov, J. *Passive- aggressive (negativistic) personality disorder.* In W. J. Livesley (Ed.), The DSM-IV Personality Disorders. New York: Guilford Press. 1995, Page 314-316.
[72] Ibid. Page 321.

develop their political and philosophical views. As a means of coping, nascent progressives displace the cause for their misery outward. By displacing these negative emotions onto the world at large, especially authority figures and their fellow citizens who possess pleasure and confidence, the progressive can temporarily fend off the abyss of self-hatred. At their core, politically active progressives are desperately trying to stay alive by destroying the societal structures and authority figures that they blame for their pervasive sense of displeasure. I'll reference again what Bill Ayers told Occupy Wall Street protesters on April 1, 2012 in Chicago, Illinois:

> "I get up every morning thinking, today I'm gonna make a difference. Today I'm gonna end capitalism. Today I'm gonna make a revolution. I go to bed every night disappointed, but I'm back again tomorrow. That's the only way you can do it." [73]

When Ayers said: "That is the only way you can do *it*," he is saying that the only way he can **emotionally survive** ("it") is to foment revolution. He needs to believe that he will end capitalism and make revolution to emotionally survive. Those

---

[73] Bill Ayers. Speaking to members of Occupy Wall Street in Chicago, Illinois. April 1, 2012.

dreams keep him going, keep him alive and keep him from falling into a desperate and bottomless despair.

Larry Grathwohl, an FBI informant who infiltrated the Weather Underground, testified under oath before a Congressional Hearing on the 60s revolutionaries in that group. He testified that Bill Ayers wanted to overthrow the United States Government and, if necessary, kill large segments of the American population. In an interview in 1982, Grathwohl said this:

> I asked them (Ayers and company) what was going to happen once they took over. The group opined that the Soviets, the North Vietnamese, China and Cuba would want to occupy certain areas of the United States. They acknowledged that re-education camps would have to be set up to reform American capitalists and freedom fighters involved in the inevitable counter-revolution. Grathwohl asked Ayers: But what are you going to do with those who resist re-education? "The thing, the most bone chilling thing Bill Ayers said to me was that after the revolution succeeded and the government was overthrown, they believed they would have to eliminate 25 million Americans who would not

conform to the new order." When I asked them what they meant by 'eliminate,' the answer was 'killed.'"

Grathwohl went on to say:

> Imagine being in a room with 25 people with graduate degrees from schools like Columbia, and other well-known colleges and universities, and they are sitting there figuring out the logistics of killing 25 million Americans.[74]

It will come as no surprise that Ayers has denied ever saying such things. For the record, Ayers has been recorded voicing his deep desire for revolution. He told children to "kill your parents" in 2001. His anarchist bombing sprees conducted when he was a young man, paired with his alliances with Communist dictators across the globe, suggests that Grathwohl's testimony is perfectly consistent with Ayers behavioral tendencies.

Theodore Millon, Ph.D., a primary author of *Axis II Disorders* (personality disorders) in the DSM series, has captured the essence of those suffering from the progressive virus:

> "For individuals with passive-aggressive (negativistic) personality disorder, being difficult, quixotic, unpredictable, and discontent produces

---

[74] Documentary Film: "No Place to Hide." An interview with FBI informant, Larry Grathwohl. 1982.

certain rewards and avoids certain discomforts. These individuals can control others by forcing them into an uncomfortable anticipatory stance. People in relationships with PAPD individuals are perpetually waiting for the next struggle, the next grievance, the next round of volatility and carping criticism. Passive-aggressive individuals are able, within their relationships, to trap people into situations wherein whatever they do is wrong. Relating to individuals with PAPD becomes a tense, edgy experience where great caution must be employed to avoid precipitating an angry incident." [75]

As the reader can surmise from Millon's description, those vulnerable to the progressive virus are just waiting for some expression or manifestation of social injustice to unleash their pent-up anger and frustration. Passive aggressive personalities can be thought of as having "hair triggers."

At their essence, progressives have deeply rooted issues with authority. On the one hand they rebel at the slightest reasonable demand or passively resist any attempt to direct them; but on the other hand, progressives are tyrannical and

---

[75] Millon, T. *Disorders of personality: DSM-III, Axis II*. New York: Wiley-Interscience. 1981, Pg. 258.

exercise group authority with ruthless and sadistic efficiency. Where does this problem with authority come from?

The origin of progressive's issues with authority can be traced to their relationship with their parents, to wit:

> "The classic passive-aggressive behaviors of being contrary, sulking, and engaging in verbal repartee can be traced back to intense power struggles with parents. The comparative helplessness of children who were also willful and stubborn made it impossible for them to win power struggles with parents and made it impossible for them to submit to their parent's authority without sulking and feeling miserable. This is especially true if their parents were overly authoritarian and unyielding. In response to authority, these nascent progressive children learned to develop passive resistance techniques. Their world is unfair, full of social injustice and their fantasies center around overthrowing their parents. [76]

The irony of these children growing up to be exactly like their parents is breathtaking.

---

[76] Stone, Michael H. Abnormalities of personality: within and beyond the realm of treatment. New York: W.W. Norton. 1993.

Progressives work in groups because they feel inadequate acting alone. One can see that mass social disobedience is tailor-made for passive aggressive personalities. They need constant reassurance but never fully trust it when they receive it. Moreover, progressives prefer to work indirectly, in a sneaky and obtuse manner. They won't disclose to the public at large what they intend to do because they fear the inevitable rejection when others discover that they are dealing with a perpetually angry and morose personalities intent upon destroying the very fiber of traditional America.

On a personal level, progressives are notoriously snarky, snide and cryptic. Their anger operates just below the surface awaiting some provocation that elicits a snide comment, mean "joke" or an outright expression of rage. Listen closely and you will hear thinly veiled anger in almost everything they say. Their micro-non-verbal expressions are replete with scowling, biting and aggressive postures.

Substance abuse in this population is rampant and it can be thought of as a form of self-medication. They feel bad and fomenting revolution can only do so much to ease the pain. When they are alone, they feel an emptiness that begs for relief. That relief is frequently found in the use of mind-altering drugs.

Many middle-aged progressives have taken LSD and other hallucinogenics. Almost all have or do smoke marijuana. These observations are corroborated by the data. ABC News investigated Baby-Boomer's abuse of drugs,

> "It turns out that those who came of age in the marijuana-happy, acid-dropping, cocaine-snorting 1960s and '70s are finding their way back to drugs.
>
> In 2010, nearly 2.4 million people ages 50 to 59 said they had abused prescription or illegal drugs within the past month; more than double that of 2002, according to data from the National Institutes of Health.
>
> Emergency rooms nationwide are seeing more patients age 55 and older for reactions to cocaine, heroin and especially marijuana.
>
> Visits to the emergency room for marijuana abuse, for example, jumped 200% from 2004 to 2009 in this age group, according to Gayathri Dowling, PhD, the acting chief of the science

policy branch at the National Institute on Drug Abuse (NIDA)." [77]

Progressives wear denim, eat lots of cruciferous vegetables, are more likely to shop at organic food markets, take vitamin and mineral supplements and use four letter words when "off camera" like a drunken sailor (with no offense to sailors).

Progressive women are strong, thin and wear short-cropped hair. Short-cropped graying hair is a style many progressive women prefer when middle-aged. The males are wispy, soft-spoken and pale. Their outward appearance hides a seething and moody Alpha-male "wanna-be" who plans, plots, schemes and spends most of his waking hours in manipulating group psychology. Progressive males despise true Alpha males.

Progressives are agnostic or atheists. This fact is often misunderstood as simply the absence of a spiritual sense or a reflection of a cognitive belief that God is a myth, created by man. But that is not the case.

Consider this, if the general population of a country believes that their fundamental rights as citizens derive from God, e.g., the God-given right to life, liberty and the pursuit of happiness, then any attempt on the part of government to either grant or

---

[77] ABC News. Back in the Habit: Baby Boomers and Drugs. Reported by Lisa Stark. August 6, 2012.

impose limitations on such inalienable rights, is met with resistance or outright rejection.

When citizens believe that their inalienable rights derive from a higher power and not bureaucrats empowered by government, those same citizens are not supplicant nor are they receptive to that which is fundamental to a socialist revolution: The submission to or reliance upon government.

Getting rid of God is a necessary and fundamental prerequisite to the progressive's grand scheme. This is why we see references to God being removed from public schools and in public displays all across the United States. This is the handiwork of progressive revolutionaries working behind the scenes. Christmas, Easter and Passover are cultural and religious events that buttress citizen's relationship with the source of their inalienable rights. Therefore, progressives must eradicate these cultural and religious celebrations so as to create a more supplicant population.

As with all progressive schemes, the true motive to remove religion and God from the public square is never said with openness and honesty. Rather, their true motives are shrouded within facades of fairness, equity or cynically, freedom of religion or separation of church and state. Once again, the irony is overwhelming.

CHAPTER NINE

The Progressive Virus in Action

California

CALIFORNIA IS ARGUABLY THE most progressive state in the union. Therefore, California is a good place to examine the progressive virus in action. One would expect to find a lot of progressive group activity in a progressive state, and that is, in fact, the case.

The state of California employs some two-and-a-quarter million people. The state has almost 400 state agencies, oversees 29 different legal codes, administers a tax code with more than 60,000 clauses or sections and spends more than $100 billion a year. The members of these various governmental agencies and bureaucracies represent a "political class" irreparably infected with the progressive virus. The "class" functions as a parasite that feels entitled to the fruits of the labor of private sector Californians.

Sacramento is crawling with more than 1,200 lobbyists whose sole job is to encourage the legislative class to redistribute wealth from California taxpayers to their clients.

Hundreds of thousands of Californians belong to public sector unions.

> "The largest numbers of union members live in California, numbering approximately 2.4 million, with New York a close second at roughly 1.9 million members. Over half of the 14.8 million union members in the U.S. lived in just seven states (California, 2.4 million; New York, 1.9 million; Illinois, 0.9 million; Pennsylvania, 0.8 million; Michigan 0.7 million; and New Jersey and Ohio, 0.6 million each), though these states accounted for only about one-third of wage and salary employment nationally." [78]

Public service unions garnish the wages of its members with mandatory dues. Those dues are then used to finance the campaigns of California politicians who, in turn, negotiate their donor's public employee compensation packages. California's progressive legislators tax the public to pay the wages of public employees who take those same taxpayer generated funds and give them back to the same politicians who in turn provide their donors with fat paychecks and fat pensions. The fact that California is broke is of little consequence to progressives who believe that they are entitled to confiscate wealth from the

---

[78] Bureau of Labor Statistics, Union Members Summary, 2011.

private sector to pay public employees. Alexis de Tocqueville said this about early America:

> **"The American Republic will endure until the day Congress discovers that it can bribe the public with the public's money."** [79]

Of course, California taxpayers are leaving the state in droves due to California's regressive tax policies. In November of 2011, L.A. Times reporters Gale Holland and Sam Quinones took note of this mass exodus.

> "[R]ecent census figures show the state is losing more Californians than it is attracting from other parts of the U.S. And the trend toward out-migration is looking less like a blip than a long-term condition. The proportion of Californians who had moved here from out of state reached a 100-year low of about 20% in 2010, and the decade measured by the most recent census was the first in a century in which the majority of Californians were native-born.
>
> The demographics of California today more closely resemble those of 1900 than of 1950: It is a mostly home-grown population, whose future

---

[79] Alexis de Tocqueville, Democracy in America,. New York: A. S. Barnes & Co., 1851.

depends on the children of immigrants and their children, said William Frey, a demographer and senior fellow at the Brookings Institution. "We used to say California, here we come," said Frey. "That now has flipped." [80]

California's budget deficit, its public teacher compensation system and its never ending quest to raise taxes on a population that is already among the highest taxed citizens in the country, are all symptoms of the progressive virus.

"In 2011 California spent more than 25.4 billion dollars *more than* it took in. California's employer-paid Unemployment Insurance Fund is insolvent. The fund had a deficit of $10.3 billion in 2010, a deficit that will rise to approximately $13.4 billion in 2011. "[81]

Democratic Governor Jerry Brown offered one solution to California's budget deficit that included increasing funding for public school teachers through higher taxes.

"Gov. Jerry Brown released a new budget Thursday that would slash health and welfare programs for the poor and ask voters to pump nearly $5 billion back into education through

---

[80] Los Angeles Times. Reporters Gale Holland and Sam Quinones, November, 2011.
[81] Capitol Weekly. Reporter Greg Lucas, March, 24, 2011.

higher taxes. Brown framed his $92.6 billion spending plan as an either-or decision dependent on his $6.9 billion initiative to increase taxes on sales and the state's high earners. If voters approve his taxes, he suggested the state could begin paying down years of debt and reverse recession-era cuts to K-12 schools, which have stuffed more students into classrooms and shortened the instructional calendar to save funds." [82]

Based upon Brown's budget, a thoughtful reader would conclude that California's teachers are under paid. In fact, California's teachers are some of the highest paid teachers in the country. Despite their high pay, California's public school student's achievement scores are near the bottom of all states. And it is not just working teachers who are highly paid; retired teachers receive fat pensions thanks to the progressive legislators in Sacramento.

"[T]he average annual salary in 2010 for active working educators enrolled in the system was $64,156. The average retirement benefit paid out in 2010 was $4,256 per month. That's $51,072 annually. In other words, the average retired

---

[82] Sacramento Bee, March 5, 2012.

teacher in California made more than the average working teacher in 28 states, according to the salary rankings published by NEA. While the value of the pension system's assets has increased fairly steadily over the past nine years, the accrued liabilities have grown non-stop during the same period, leaving the fund at 78% of full coverage. What's more, CalSTRS operated on an assumed annual return of 8 percent. Last year, the pension board lowered that expectation to 7.75 percent, which means projections for the future will show even more of a gap." [83]

Governor Jerry Brown could be a poster child for what a progressive viral infection creates. He and his fellow progressive infected legislators believe that social justice demands reallocation of wealth. Governments achieve this reallocation through higher taxes and more regulation. Wealthy Californians are viewed as oppressors. Therefore, their money is assumed to NOT be the product of hard work, talent, industry and risk, but as a consequence of inheritance, oppression of the have-nots and/or luck.

In the most progressive state in the union resides the most progressive city in the United States. San Francisco is a sanctuary

---

[83] California State Teachers' Retirement System (CalSTRS), 2010.

city for illegal aliens. It is also a city that tried to outlaw circumcisions and outlaws gold fish. Throwing orange peels, coffee grounds and grease-stained pizza boxes in the trash is also against the law in San Francisco. San Francisco is deeply concerned about obesity, so it has outlawed McDonald's Happy Meals. San Francisco Supervisor Eric Mar, who sponsored the Unhappy Meals legislation, praised its potential impact on the obesity problem.

> "We're part of a movement that is moving forward an agenda of food justice," Mar said in a prepared statement late Tuesday. "From San Francisco to New York City, the epidemic of childhood obesity in this country is making our kids sick, particularly kids from low-income neighborhoods, at an alarming rate. It's a survival issue and a day-to-day issue." [84]

On the other hand, try to pass a law that prohibits gay men from sitting their naked derrieres down in restaurants and the city erupts in protest.

> "It used to be that there would be one nude guy wandering around the neighborhood and no one thought twice about it," said Mr. Wiener, who

---

[84] Market Watch, *Health Matters*, Reporter Kristine Gerenchers, November 9, 2010.

represents the city's Castro district. "Now it's a regular thing and much more obnoxious. We have guys sitting down naked in public without the common decency to put something down underneath them." [85]

In response to the proposed law a "nude in" protest took place in the Castro District.

California is where those infected with the progressive virus moved to and those who had some immunity to the virus fled. California's public schools and its economic woes are the direct result of the golden state's infection with the progressive virus that has all but nullified Horace Greely's edict, "Go West Youngman."

Certainly with all of this civic concern for the welfare of its citizens, San Francisco's public school students must be doing very well. Think again.

"Eighty percent of San Francisco public schools failed to make adequate yearly progress as defined by the federal No Child Left Behind law, the California Department of Education announced Wednesday. The district as a whole also did not meet targets for students passing math and English tests, though it did meet a

---

[85] New York Times. Reporter: Malia Wollan September 25, 2011.

target for graduation, with 86 percent of students leaving high school with a diploma. Though most San Francisco schools did not meet federal requirements, the district did gain five points on California's own Academic Performance Index, or API, earning a score of 796. That is just four points shy of the state's target. Statewide, only 35 percent of elementary schools, 18 percent of middle schools and 41 percent of high schools met No Child Left Behind target, a decline of 5 percentage points for elementaries, 8 points for middle schools and 1 point for high schools. "[86]

"California ranks near the bottom of all states in the number of students reaching their educational goals. California students generally have lower test scores than students across the nation. White students in California also perform well below white students in almost all other states. In 2006, only two-thirds of ninth grade students went on to graduate. Two-thirds of the state's schools fail to offer enough classes to qualify students to even apply to college.

---

[86] San Francisco Examiner. Reporter Amy Crawford August 31, 2011.

Studying the 2006 class of high school graduates in California, less than one-third went to community college, only one in nine went to California State campuses and fewer than one in 12 went on to a University of California campus."[87]

While progressives in San Francisco regulate Happy Meals, Goldfish, and defend their gay citizen's right to walk around nude, 80% of San Francisco's public school students fail to make the grade.

But other problems directly linked to the progressive virus are undermining the "Golden State's" most progressive city. National Geographic highlighted San Francisco in its documentary on the drug crystal methamphetamine.

"**Narrator:** When it comes to crack there's one pleasure that is heightened more than any other...sex. The health impact on some communities is extreme. San Francisco is a Mecca for gay, lesbian and bi-sexual people from all over the world. In a community that has suffered the terrible effects of HIV and AIDS, methamphetamine has taken a strong hold with dire consequences for those fighting the HIV virus.

---

[87] UCLA's Institute for Democracy, Education and Access (IDEA), John Rogers Director, 2009. As reported in UCLA Today, reporter Judy Lin, February 23, 2009.

Since the mid 90s, crystal meth has been the drug of choice in the gay club scene. Aaron Schirmer took many drugs, including heroin, before he discovered meth. He was part of San Francisco's gay crystal meth scene for 8 years.

Schirmer: Crystal meth is very accessible. You can walk down the street and buy crystal meth you know, and most of the gay communities. On the weekends it's really easy to find in clubs. Uh, you know, I used to go into bars and stand in the restroom and be offered a line.

Narrator: Crystal meth gives users a rush of energy. The cascade of dopamine entering the brain and central nervous system also intensifies feeling of sexual arousal.

Schirmer: I get an amazing and euphoric rush, like you know, I'm experiencing primal like, you know, urges that I've always wanted to feel.

Narrator: Aaron, a photographer and club D.J., has been HIV positive since he was 15. Unsafe sex is usually fraught with the danger of infecting someone. But when he is injecting or slamming methamphetamine, sex suddenly becomes uninhibited and guilt free.

Schirmer: I had the kind of sex that you would have pre-HIV, you know, its like where you could take all your clothes off, be totally naked and be your all with someone. Losing all your inhibitions like that feels really amazing.

Narrator: Many HIV positive men in the city end up having unprotected sex with one another.

Schirmer: You have to take the population of people who shoot crystal meth or who use crystal meth, who are all HIV, and so that sex pool, that pool of people, you know can all have sex with each other and not worry about transmission to one another which is, in some ways has been kind of like a beautiful part of it, of the crystal meth scene.

Narrator: Crystal meth soon becomes more than just a club drug, homosexual meth users turn to internet dating sites to hook up, and the search term "party n' play" or P n' P becomes code for drug fueled sex.

Gay Man: If you put P n' P people together who are interested in doing crystal meth and having sex, you know, it's kind of like a fast food version food and sex and drugs. You can get high and have someone at your door within minutes with drugs and ready to have sex with you.

Narrator: For those high on drugs, practicing safe sex is often forgotten in the haze.

Gay Man: You can get high after some meth and party all night long, and partying all night long can mean having sex with lots of guys all night long, even days on end, and the drug keeps you high for that long, and um, and I personally, would often, what happens is that using any kind of protection kind of goes out the window.

Narrator: When HIV negative men join in, the crystal meth craze becomes even more deadly.

Schirmer: You have the people who are new, coming into the crystal meth scene who lose all their inhibitions that are HIV negative who are really vulnerable and especially when you have, like you know, HIV'ers and non-HIV'ers all shooting up and all losing inhibitions at once.

Narrator: Of the 28,000 cases of AIDS diagnosed in San Francisco for 2008, ¾ were among men who have sex with other men.

Within this community, crystal meth is now a major driver for new HIV infection.

Gay Man: If you use methamphetamine you are 3 to 4 times more likely to have HIV than gay men who don't, so I mean, it's really a significant part of why HIV infections continue to occur.

Narrator: Despite the risk, the pleasures that come with crystal make it extremely hard to give up.

Schirmer: It is the most psychologically addictive drug I've ever taken in my life and to this day getting off crystal meth is a lot harder than getting off heroin.

Narrator: The overall cost of methamphetamine to the United States is estimated at $23 billion dollars a year. But the human cost of the ruined relationships, careers and health of addicts is impossible to quantify. Even so, $35 billion dollars worth of profits from producing and distributing meth continue to pour into drugs incorporated. "[88]

The San Francisco residents highlighted in National Geographic's documentary on crystal methamphetamine are the constituents of California's 8th Congressional District. Former

---

[88] National Geographic. Drugs, Inc. Crystal Methamphetamine. 2011.

Speaker of the House, and now minority leader, Nancy Pelosi, represents that district in the Congress. These are her people.

It was Speaker Pelosi who ram-rodded through the House The Patient Protection and Affordable Care Act, aka "ObamaCare." It was former Speaker Pelosi who was front and center at the unofficial hearing featuring Sandra Fluke and it was Nancy Pelosi who granted numerous waivers to AFL/CIO members for participation in ObamaCare and also praised the First Lady, Michele Obama, for her focus upon childhood obesity.

Nancy Pelosi condemns high fat diets and approves of virtually every nanny-state regulation proposed or enacted that limits the kinds and types of cooking oils, salt and calorie content found in food. She is a "warrior" in the war on obesity. On the other hand, she favors providing free birth control to students in elite Catholic schools and supports gay men's "right" to display their genitalia in public during "celebrations" of gay pride along with everyday displays of nudity on public streets in plain view of children. But the rampant HIV infection rates and out of control drug abuse in her own Congressional district fail to show up on her radar. Former speaker Pelosi is as quiet as a church mouse when it comes to calling out her constituents for costing the rest of America millions upon millions of dollars in health care costs related to discretionary personal behavior that impacts all American taxpayers.

CHAPTER TEN

The Progressive Virus in Action

The Transportation Security Administration (TSA)

ANOTHER CLASSIC EXAMPLE OF the progressive virus in action is the Transportation Security Administration (TSA). The TSA and its practices are a reflection of progressive dogma. Screening protocols that make use of intelligent profiling (The approach used by Israel) to discriminate between high and low risk groups and individuals is banned. The agency denies that such differences exist between groups or individuals on the dimension of threat. As a result, 90 year-old Anglo-European wheelchair-bound Americans are screened no differently than 22 year-old Yemeni Muslims who are flying with a one-way ticket paid in cash.

Accurate profiling is something that every human must do to stay alive. Inaccurate profiling is bad, accurate profiling is necessary for survival. We all profile on a daily basis. Imagine you are a young African-American male walking down a street. You notice a huge Rottweiler dog with a spiked collar trotting toward you. The dog is accompanied by an African American male who has a menacing look on his face. Now imagine that same street, only this time approaching you is an older neighbor lady walking her toy-poodle on a leash. Are you going to profile one dog over another?

The most progressive Anglo person in the country is not likely to walk in Harlem late at night, but he probably would go for a stroll late at night at "Downtown Disney" in Anaheim, California. That's accurate profiling. By choosing not to walk alone in Los Angeles's Watts District, The Southside of Chicago or Harlem, the person making that choice has profiled a location and the residents of that part of the city as representing a disproportionately high threat to their personal safety.

Let's say you are the famous director Spike Lee, is it risky for you to go for a walk at night in Downtown Detroit, Michigan without a film crew and security personnel in tow? Is it smart to profile that city and its residents? Should you profile that city and its residents?

According to FBI statistics, the Detroit metropolitan area (Detroit-Livonia-Dearborn) was the most dangerous city in the United States for the year 2010. The high murder rate helped make the Motor City the most violent crime-prone area in the United States in 2010, with 1,111 violent crimes reported per 100,000 residents. [89]

---

[89] Forbes Magazine. America's Most Dangerous Cities. October 3, 2011.

A western female journalist who chooses not to walk alone in Iraq is engaged in profiling, as is a person in need of medical care who chooses a hospital frequented by movie stars and world-leaders to receive care. When a taller more athletic person is chosen in a pick-up basketball game over a shorter, less athletic person, that's profiling.

Choosing Captain "Sully" as your pilot over a very young, inexperienced, giddy and slovenly dressed pilot, is smart profiling. If you are a person who panhandles, approaching another panhandler for a handout is not as smart as approaching a well-dressed friendly looking pedestrian for a handout. That's smart profiling.

Testosterone-laden males between the ages of 18 and 35, who are covered in gang-affiliated tattoos, who are walking toward you with an aggressive non-verbal posture, should be profiled differently on the dimension of threat when compared to a group of older Black women between the ages of 50 and 85, coming home from a church service with their bibles in hand and wearing their Sunday best. That's accurate profiling and it's smart. If you are a police officer do you view young Hispanics dressed in gang affiliated wear with MS-13 tattoos on their bodies driving in a neighborhood late at night with their headlights off the same way you view a group of older women coming out a church parking lot with their headlights off? If you say there is no difference or if you contend that there should be no distinctions made, you have proven yourself to be hopelessly infected with the progressive virus.

Inaccurate, but understandable and innocent profiling should be distinguished from inaccurate profiling. Let's say that you are performing at a local theater. You are playing the role of a murderous thug in an urban drama about life on the streets. After the performance you walk out of the theater in full wardrobe on your way to a cast party a few blocks from the theater. A couple of blocks away from the theater you are stopped by a police officer that wants to know who you are and what you are doing. The actor "looks like" a suspect in the area who has been responsible for multiple rapes. This is understandable and innocent, but it is inaccurate profiling.

Many young men have adopted a style of fashion that mimics prison garb and gang affiliated clothes. Very baggy pants, for example, make it very easy to hide a weapon. Wearing a "hoodie" is a criminal's most favored means of making it difficult to identify him. Criminal defense lawyers love the fact that their defendant clients were reported as wearing a hoodie by eye-witnesses.

Should people wearing hoodies be profiled? A person wearing a hoodie on a hot day, late at night, loitering around a convenience store, should garner special attention. A person wearing a hoodie on a cold night, walking in a well-lit area should not, necessarily, garner special attention.

I have a friend who loves to wear full-length capes on cold days. When she shops she will wear her cape and when she enters the store she used to put her purse under her cape to keep it safe. The first time I saw this I explained to her that she would garner unnecessary attention because she looked like she was hiding something under her cape. My friend had never stolen anything in her life. After being shadowed by store security and stopped a few times as she was leaving the clothing store, she stopped wearing her cape while shopping. She had been inaccurately profiled, but understandably so. Should she have been offended? Should store security stop looking closely at people with bulges under their full capes?

According to the Federal Bureau of Prisons, there are 217,247 inmates as of March 24 of 2012. Want to guess what percentage of those inmates are male? Before you answer, ask yourself if even asking that question is profiling? The answer is this: Of the 217,247 inmates residing in Federal prisons in the United States, 203,186 are male, or 93.5%. [90] Does this mean that males are being profiled? Can one take a data point like this and reverse engineer it to the conclusion that because the vast

---

[90] United States Department of Justice. Federal Bureau of Prisons. March 24, 2012.

majority of federal inmates are male that males are being profiled, that women are getting a "pass" from law enforcement and the courts? The answer is no. Males pose a greater risk of committing a federal crime.

What follows is a history of major terrorist attacks over the last 33 years. Do you see a consistent pattern?

1979

> **Nov. 4, Tehran, Iran:** Iranian radical students seized the U.S. embassy, taking 66 hostages. 14 were later released. The remaining 52 were freed after 444 days on the day of President Reagan's inauguration.

1982–1991

> **Lebanon:** Thirty US and other Western hostages kidnapped in Lebanon by Hezbollah. Some were killed, some died in captivity, and some were eventually released. Terry Anderson was held for 2,454 days.

1983

> **April 18, Beirut, Lebanon:** U.S. embassy destroyed in suicide car-bomb attack; 63 dead, including 17 Americans. The Islamic Jihad claimed responsibility.
>
> **Oct. 23, Beirut, Lebanon:** Shiite suicide bombers exploded truck near U.S. military barracks at Beirut airport, killing 241 marines. Minutes later a second bomb killed 58 French paratroopers in their barracks in West Beirut.
>
> **Dec. 12, Kuwait City, Kuwait:** Shiite truck bombers attacked the U.S. embassy and other targets, killing 5 and injuring 80.

1984

> **Sept. 20, East Beirut, Lebanon:** truck bomb exploded outside the U.S. embassy annex, killing 24, including 2 U.S. military.

Dec. 3, Beirut, Lebanon: Kuwait Airways Flight 221, from Kuwait to Pakistan, hijacked and diverted to Tehran. 2 Americans killed.

1985

April 12, Madrid, Spain: Bombing at restaurant frequented by U.S. soldiers, killed 18 Spaniards and injured 82.

June 14, Beirut, Lebanon: TWA Flight 847 en route from Athens to Rome hijacked to Beirut by Hezbollah terrorists and held for 17 days. A U.S. Navy diver executed.

Oct. 7, Mediterranean Sea: gunmen attack Italian cruise ship, *Achille Lauro*. One U.S. tourist killed. Hijacking linked to Libya.

Dec. 18, Rome, Italy, and Vienna, Austria: airports in Rome and Vienna were bombed, killing 20 people, 5 of whom were Americans. Bombing linked to Libya.

1986

April 2, Athens, Greece:A bomb exploded aboard TWA flight 840 en route from Rome to Athens, killing 4 Americans and injuring 9.

April 5, West Berlin, Germany: Libyans bombed a disco frequented by U.S. servicemen, killing 2 and injuring hundreds.

1988

Dec. 21, Lockerbie, Scotland: N.Y.-bound Pan-Am Boeing 747 exploded in flight from a terrorist bomb and crashed into Scottish village, killing all 259 aboard and 11 on the ground. Passengers included 35 Syracuse University students and many U.S. military personnel. Libya formally admitted responsibility 15 years later (Aug. 2003) and offered $2.7 billion compensation to victims' families.

1993

Feb. 26, New York City: bomb exploded in basement garage of World Trade Center, killing 6 and injuring at least 1,040 others. In 1995, militant Islamist Sheik Omar

Abdel Rahman and 9 others were convicted of conspiracy charges, and in 1998, Ramzi Yousef, believed to have been the mastermind, was convicted of the bombing. Al-Qaeda involvement is suspected.

1995

April 19, Oklahoma City: car bomb exploded outside federal office building, collapsing wall and floors. 168 people were killed, including 19 children and 1 person who died in rescue effort. Over 220 buildings sustained damage. Timothy McVeigh and Terry Nichols later convicted in the antigovernment plot to avenge the Branch Davidian standoff in Waco, Tex., exactly 2 years earlier.

Nov. 13, Riyadh, Saudi Arabia: car bomb exploded at U.S. military headquarters, killing 5 U.S. military servicemen.

1996

June 25, Dhahran, Saudi Arabia: truck bomb exploded outside Khobar Towers military complex, killing 19 American servicemen and injuring hundreds of others. 13 Saudis and a Lebanese, all alleged members of Islamic militant group Hezbollah, were indicted on charges relating to the attack in June 2001.

1998

Aug. 7, Nairobi, Kenya, and Dar es Salaam, Tanzania: truck bombs exploded almost simultaneously near 2 U.S. embassies, killing 224 (213 in Kenya and 11 in Tanzania) and injuring about 4,500. 4 men connected with al-Qaeda 2 of whom had received training at al-Qaeda camps inside Afghanistan, were convicted of the killings in May 2001 and later sentenced to life in prison. A federal grand jury had indicted 22 men in connection with the attacks, including Saudi dissident Osama bin Laden, who remained at large.

2000

Oct. 12, Aden, Yemen: U.S. Navy destroyer USS *Cole* heavily damaged when a small boat loaded with explosives blew up alongside it. 17 sailors killed. Linked to Osama bin Laden, or members of al-Qaeda terrorist network.

2001

Sept. 11, New York City, Arlington, Va., and Shanksville, Pa.: hijackers crashed 2 commercial jets into twin towers of World Trade Center; 2 more hijacked jets were crashed into the Pentagon and a field in rural Pa. Total dead and missing numbered 2,992[1]: 2,749 in New York City, 184 at the Pentagon, 40 in Pa., and 19 hijackers. Islamic al-Qaeda terrorist group blamed. (*See* September 11, 2001: Timeline of Terrorism.)

2002

June 14, Karachi, Pakistan: bomb explodes outside American consulate in Karachi, Pakistan, killing 12. Linked to al-Qaeda.

2003 [1]

May 12, Riyadh, Saudi Arabia: suicide bombers kill 34, including 8 Americans, at housing compounds for Westerners. Al-Qaeda suspected.

2004

May 29–31, Riyadh, Saudi Arabia: terrorists attack the offices of a Saudi oil company in Khobar, Saudi Arabia, take foreign oil workers hostage in a nearby residential compound, leaving 22 people dead including one American.

June 11–19, Riyadh, Saudi Arabia: terrorists kidnap and execute Paul Johnson Jr., an American, in Riyadh, Saudi Arabia. 2 other Americans and BBC cameraman killed by gun attacks.

Dec. 6, Jeddah, Saudi Arabia: terrorists storm the U.S. consulate, killing 5 consulate employees. 4 terrorists were killed by Saudi security.

2005

Nov. 9, Amman, Jordan: suicide bombers hit 3 American hotels, Radisson, Grand Hyatt, and Days Inn, in Amman, Jordan, killing 57. Al-Qaeda claimed responsibility.

2006

Sept. 13, Damascus, Syria: an attack by four gunman on the American embassy is foiled.

2007

Jan. 12, Athens, Greece: the U.S. embassy is fired on by an anti-tank missile causing damage but no injuries.

Dec. 11, Algeria: more than 60 people are killed, including 11 United Nations staff members, when Al Qaeda terrorists detonate two car bombs near Algeria's Constitutional Council and the United Nations offices.

2008

May 26, Iraq: a suicide bomber on a motorcycle kills six U.S. soldiers and wounds 18 others in Tarmiya.

June 24, Iraq: a suicide bomber kills at least 20 people, including three U.S. Marines, at a meeting between sheiks and Americans in Karmah, a town west of Baghdad.

June 12, Afghanistan: four American servicemen are killed when a roadside bomb explodes near a U.S. military vehicle in Farah Province.

July 13, Afghanistan: nine U.S.soldiers and at least 15 NATO troops die when Taliban militants boldly attack an American base in Kunar Province, which borders Pakistan. It's the most deadly against U.S. troops in three years.

Aug. 18 and 19, Afghanistan: as many as 15 suicide bombers backed by about 30 militants attack a U.S. military base, Camp Salerno, in Bamiyan. Fighting between U.S. troops and members of the Taliban rages overnight. No U.S. troops are killed.

Sept. 16, Yemen: a car bomb and a rocket strike the U.S. embassy in Yemen as staff arrived to work, killing 16 people, including 4 civilians. At least 25 suspected al-Qaeda militants are arrested for the attack.

Nov. 26, India: in a series of attacks on several of Mumbai's landmarks and commercial hubs that are popular with Americans and other foreign tourists, including at least two five-star hotels, a hospital, a train station, and a cinema. About 300 people are wounded and nearly 190 people die, including at least 5 Americans.

2009

Feb. 9, Iraq: a suicide bomber kills four American soldiers and their Iraqi translator near a police checkpoint.

April 10, Iraq: a suicide attack kills five American soldiers and two Iraqi policemen.

June 1, Little Rock, Arkansas: Abdulhakim Muhammed, a Muslim convert from Memphis, Tennessee, is charged with shooting two soldiers outside a military recruiting center. One is killed and the other is wounded. In a January 2010 letter to the judge hearing his case, Muhammed asked to change his plea from not guilty to guilty, claimed ties to al-Qaeda, and called the shooting a jihadi attack "to fight those who wage war on Islam and Muslims."

Dec. 25: A Nigerian man on a flight from Amsterdam to Detroit attempted to ignite an explosive device hidden in his underwear. The explosive device that failed to detonate was a mixture of powder and liquid that did not alert security personnel in the airport. The alleged bomber, Umar Farouk Abdulmutallab, told officials later that he was directed by the terrorist group Al Qaeda. The suspect was already on the government's watch list when he attempted the bombing; his father, a respected

Nigerian banker, had told the U.S. government that he was worried about his son's increased extremism.

Dec. 30, Iraq: a suicide bomber kills eight Americans civilians, seven of them CIA agents, at a base in Afghanistan. It's the deadliest attack on the agency since 9/11. The attacker is reportedly a double agent from Jordan who was acting on behalf of al-Qaeda.

2010

May 1, New York City: a car bomb is discovered in Times Square, New York City after smoke is seen coming from a vehicle. The bomb was ignited, but failed to detonate and was disarmed before it could cause any harm. Times Square was evacuated as a safety precaution. Faisal Shahzad pleads guilty to placing the bomb as well as 10 terrorism and weapons charges.

May 10, Jacksonville, Florida: a pipe bomb explodes while approximately 60 Muslims are praying in the mosque. The attack causes no injuries.

Oct. 29: two packages are found on separate cargo planes. Each package contains a bomb consisting of 300 to 400 grams (11-14 oz) of plastic explosives and a detonating mechanism. The bombs are discovered as a result of intelligence received from Saudi Arabia's security chief. The packages, bound from Yemen to the United States, are discovered at en route stop-overs, one in England and one in Dubai in the United Arab Emirates.

2011

Jan. 17, Spokane, Washington: a pipe bomb is discovered along the route of the Martin Luther King, Jr. memorial march. The bomb, a "viable device" set up to spray marchers with shrapnel and to cause multiple casualties, is defused without any injuries.

Since 9/11 there have been at least 45 deadly terrorist attacks that were thwarted by various intelligence agencies. Here is the list as of 2011:

1. Richard Reid December 2001

Shoe bomber.

2. 'Library Tower' Plot February 2002

Plot to attempt a second 9/11-style aerial attack to topple the tallest building in Los Angeles.

3. José Padilla May 2002

Accused of meeting with Khalid Sheikh Mohammed in a dirty bomb plot. Sentenced to 17 years in 2008.

4. Earnest James Ujaama July 2002

Seattle-based terror cell plotted to support the Taliban.

5. U.S. Forces in Germany September 2002

A man and a woman of Turkish heritage—the man born in Germany—are arrested for plotting to blow up U.S. Army headquarters in Germany.

6. Lackawanna Cell September 2002

Six Yemeni-Americans are <u>accused of</u> conspiring to help al Qaeda and plead guilty.

7. Oregon Taliban Plot October 2002

Seven Oregonians <u>arrested</u> in plot to join the Taliban and wage war against the United States.

8. Al Qaeda Gas Attack Plot on NYC Subways Spring 2003

<u>Reported by</u> Ron Suskind in *The One Percent Doctrine*.

9. Iyman Farris May 2003

Plot to <u>destroy</u> the Brooklyn Bridge.

10. Virginia Jihad Network June 2003

Virginia group <u>trained for</u> apparent urban warfare missions, including training in Afghanistan.

11. Nuradin M. Abdi November 2003

Plotted <u>to bomb</u> a Columbus, Ohio, shopping mall.

12. Dhiren Barot August 2004

Plotted <u>to bomb</u> locations in New York, Newark, and Washington.

13. James Elshafay and Shahawar Matin Siraj August 2004

Plotted to bomb train station near Madison Square Garden in bid to disrupt the Republican National Convention.

14. Levar Haley Washington, Gregory Vernon Patterson, Hammad Riaz Samana, and Kevin James August 2005

Arrested for conspiring to attack National Guard facilities and synagogues around Los Angeles.

15. Mohammad Zaki Amawi, Marwan Othman El-Hindi, and Zand Wassim Mazlou February 2006

Convicted in 2008 (PDF) of conspiring to commit terrorism against Americans overseas.

16. Syed Haris Ahmed and Ehsanul Islam Sadequee April 2006

Gathered surveillance and met with other terrorists about targets in Washington, D.C.

17. Narseal Batiste, Patrick Abraham, Stanley Grant Phanor, Naudimar Herrera, Burson Augustin, Lyglenson Lemorin, and Rotschild Augustine June 2006

Plotted to blow up Sears Tower.

18. Assem Hammoud July 2006

Plotted to attack PATH trains between New York and New Jersey.

19. Jetliner bombing plot August 2006

Twenty-four suspects arrested for <u>plotting to blow up</u> 10 U.S. jetliners with liquid explosives. This plot led to the regulation of liquids on planes.

20. Houston Taliban November 2006

<u>Kobie Diallo Williams</u> and four other men are charged with conspiring to support the Taliban after training in Texas.

21. Derrick Shareef December 2006

<u>Planned to</u> set off grenades at a shopping mall near Chicago.

22. Fort Dix Plot May 2007

The "<u>Fort Dix Six</u>" plotted to attack Fort Dix in New Jersey.**23. JFK Airport June 2007**

Four men plotted to <u>blow up</u> fuel tanks and pipelines at JFK Airport in New York.

24. Ramstein Air Base, Germany September 2007

German converts to Islam, plotting under the cover of the Islamic Jihad Union, are <u>found to have</u> explosives and plan to target one of the largest U.S. air bases in Europe.

25. Columbus, Ohio June 2008

Christopher Paul aka Abdul Malek, aka Paul Kenyatta Laws

Pleaded guilty to conspiring with others to blow up targets in the U.S. and Europe.

26. NYC Subway Bombing Sept. 14, 2009

Najibullah Zazi and three other men are caught days before they detonate explosives in the New York City subway.

27. Long Island Railroad Threat November 2008

American Bryant Neal Vinas gives al Qaeda leaders information to attack the LIRR.

28. Springfield, Illinois Courthouse Bomb Plot Sept. 24, 2009

Michael Finton

Arrested in plot to detonate a vehicle bomb outside a courthouse and kill federal employees.

29. Dallas Tower Plot Sept. 24, 2009

Hosam Maher Husein Smadi

A Jordanian man is arrested in connection with a plot to bomb at a skyscraper in Dallas.

30. Quantico, VA Sept. 24, 2009

Daniel Patrick Boyd

A group of men are <u>charged</u> in plot to attack the Marine Corps base in Quantico.

31. Boston October 2009

Tarek Mehanna and Ahmad Abousamra

Two men are arrested on <u>wide-ranging charges</u>, including conspiracy to kill U.S. politicians, spanning the past decade.

32. Northern Virginia December 2009

Five men from northern Virginia are <u>arrested in Pakistan</u> and charged with supporting al Qaeda. Were reported missing by their families.

33. Detroit Airspace Christmas Day Bomber, 2009

A man tries to <u>detonate an explosive</u> on a flight over Detroit. Also known as the underwear bomber.

34. Chicago March 2010

Raja Lahrasib Khan

Man is arrested for funneling money to terrorist organizations.

35. Times Square, New York City May 1, 2010

Faisal Shahzad

<u>Failed attempt</u> to detonate a vehicle bomb in Times Square.

36. King Salmon, Alaska July/August, 2010

Paul G. Rockwood, Jr. and Nadia Piroska Maria Rockwood

A husband and wife compile a list of <u>20 targets to murder</u>, including military and media figures, arrested as they were set to move into the operational phase.

37. Wrigley Field, Chicago Sept. 20, 2010

A man is arrested after <u>planting a fake bomb</u> outside Wrigley Field.

38. Air-Cargo Bomb Yemen to Chicago October 2010

Twin packages of explosives were <u>shipped</u> from Yemen to synagogues in Chicago.

39. Washington, D.C. October 2010

Farooque Ahmed

Ahmed is <u>arrested</u> in connection with a plot to blow up the D.C. Metro.

40. Portland, Oregon Nov. 26, 2010

Mohamed Osman Mohamud

A Christmas-tree lighting is <u>targeted</u> by a 19-year-old Somali man, Mohamed Osman Mohamud, busted in an FBI sting operation.

41. Catonsville, Md. Dec. 8, 2010

Antonio Martinez

Man arrested for <u>plotting to</u> blow up a U.S. Army recruiting center.

42. Lubbock, Texas/National Feb. 23, 2011

Khalid Ali-M Aldawsari

Man arrested in <u>bomb plot</u> against military and political targets, including former President George W. Bush, in New York, Colorado, and California.

43. New York City May 11, 2011

Ahmed Ferhani and Mohamed Mamdouh

Two men arrested in <u>plot to attack</u> a Manhattan synagogue.

44. Seattle, Wash. June 22, 2011 (arrest date)

Abu Khalid Abdul-Latif, aka Joseph Anthony Davis, and Walli Mujahidh

Two men are <u>arrested</u> in a plot to attack a military recruiting station in Seattle.

45. Fort Hood, Texas July 27, 2011 (arrest date)

Pfc. Naser Jason Abdo

A former army private is <u>arrested</u> in a plot to copycat attack at Fort Hood. [91]

Below is a listing of the names of the terrorists who perpetrated the attacks on September 11, 2001:

AA Flight 11
First plane sacrificed; hit the North Tower of the WTC

- Walid Al Shehri
- Wail Alsheri (aka Waleed Alsheri)
- Mohammad Atta
- Aabdul Alomari
- Satam Sugami

UA Flight 175
Second plane sacrificed; hit the South Tower of the WTC

- Marawn Alshehhi

---

[91] Dahl, Erik, J. "The Plots That Failed: Intelligence Lessons Learned From Unsuccessful Terrorist Attacks Against the United States." Studies in Conflict and Terrorism. Volume 34, Issue 8, 2011, pages 621'-648.

- Fayez Ahmed
- Mohald Alshehri
- Hamza Al Ghamdi
- Ahmed Al Ghamdi

AA Flight 77
Third plane sacrificed; hit the Pentagon

- Khalid Almihdhar
- Majed Moqued
- Nawaf Al Hazmi
- Salem Al Hazmi

UA Flight 93
Fourth plane sacrificed; crashed into the ground in Pennsylvania

- Ahmed Al Haznawi
- Ahmed Alnami
- Ziad Jarrah
- Saeed Alghamdi

Again I ask: Do you see a pattern? The progressive virus mandates that its victim declare that no differences exist between groups or individuals when it comes to the threat of committing terrorist acts against Americans or its allies.

Progressive apologists trot out Timothy McVeigh when confronted with the above data with monotonous predictability, as if that proves their convenient equilibrium thesis. That is like trotting out Muggsy Bogues [92] in response to someone who dares to assert that NBA players are taller than most Americans.

Along with McVeigh, progressive apologists conflate those suffering from paranoid schizophrenia or similar psychosis or mental illness, e.g., Jared Loughner, James Holmes or Wade Michael Page, with global, theo-political terrorism. Loughner and Holmes were victims of their own psychosis, a mental illness that became everyone's problem when their mental disorder reached critical mass. In the instance of Loughner, his psychosis erupted in Tuscon, Arizona and resulted in the murder or attempted murder of 19 people, including Congressperson Gabby Giffords. Holmes, infamous for his mug shot displaying his tattered orange, Joker-like hair, went on a shooting rampage in an Aurora, Colorado movie theater premiering the Batman movie: *The Dark Knight Rises.* Page was a "one off" neo-Nazi who attacked a group of people not like him, who happened to attend a Sikh temple in Page's neighborhood. Loughner, Holmes and Page should not be conflated with the orchestrated, theo-political aspirations of any number of nation-states in the Middle East. The agents of that movement are not psychotic, nor are they engaged in "one off" acts of brutality. Jihadists are

---

[92] Tyrone Curtis, aka, Muggsy Bogues, was the shortest player ever, at 5' 3", to play in the NBA.

dedicated and true believers, intent upon terrorizing enemy nations and their citizens.

Progressive victims routinely cite data from the FBI that allegedly show that 94% or so of all terrorist acts are NOT committed by Muslims. The FBI data that appear to show that only 6% or so of terrorist acts are committed by Muslims, includes terrorist attacks on automobile dealerships by anti-capitalists, attacks on animal experimentation labs and gang activity in Puerto Rico. FBI data categorize generic "shootings" and "robberies" as terrorist acts.

According to the FBI data cited by progressives, intended to prove that no one groups poses a special threat to the flying public, Latinos commit 42% of all terrorist attacks. Really? The FBI categorizes Latino gang violence as acts of terrorism on par with the 9/11 attacks.

Jews are said to commit 7% of all terrorist attacks, one percent higher than Muslims, according to FBI data. Jewish extremists, to my knowledge, have never attacked the flying public in America. The FBI data from 1980 to 2005, the same data relied upon by progressives, identify the highest number of terrorist attacks on U.S. soil is in Puerto Rico, a country awash in partisan strife and local conflict.

Reason and logic would demand that the TSA should remove from their screening equation the threat experienced by automobile dealerships selling gas-guzzling SUVs, animal experimentation labs and any number of other partisan targets that do NOT impact the flying public or, for that matter, the American public as a whole. Gang violence between "Crips" and "Bloods" doesn't impact the flying public. MS 13 is not targeting "infidels" on their flight to New York from Los Angeles. Puerto Rican gang violence data should not be a part of the denominator in TSA's metric on threat.

Those infected with the progressive virus, however, are implored to not make distinctions between any group, culture or individual. The progressive virus denies its victim the ability to discriminate between an act of violence against an automobile dealership, whaling vessel or townhome development, from the soldiers of Islam intent upon terrorizing Americans because we are infidels, have invaded their territories, support Israel, etc. Progressives rabidly deny the obvious in favor of confirming, even if they have to rely upon spurious data comparisons, that all peoples and cultures are equally predisposed to harm the flying public.

Imagine if during H.G. Wells "War of the Worlds," those infected with the progressive virus had been confronted with the obvious taking place before their eyes. The progressive infected and vested mass media would have trotted out a news report of an assault in Kentucky between the Hatfields and the

McCoys to prove that singling-out Martians as an existential threat to Earthlings was racist or an expression of cultural discrimination. Imagine a scene in War of the Worlds in an American airport where a little green Martian, antennae flicking back and forth, was screened no differently than a 6 year-old child walking on crutches. Sound incredible? That is exactly the scene taking place in airports all across the United States thanks to the distortions created by the progressive virus.

OK, you agree that there may be a disproportionate threat coming from some groups, but the threat is limited to "radical" Islamic terrorists. Surely, "moderate" Muslims around the world have no sympathy for acts of terrorism directed at the West, right? Take a look at the following data with regard to how average, "moderate" Muslims feel about acts of Jihadist terrorism. Each data entry includes a link to the source of the data:

ICM Poll: 20% of British Muslims sympathize with 7/7 bombers
http://www.telegraph.co.uk/news/uknews/1510866/Poll-reveals-40pc-of-Muslims-want-sharia-law-in-UK.html
NOP Research: 1 in 4 British Muslims say 7/7 bombings were justified
http://www.cbsnews.com/stories/2006/08/14/opinion/main1893879.shtml&date=2011-04-06
http://www.webcitation.org/5xkMGAEvY
People-Press: 31% of Turks support suicide attacks against Westerners in Iraq.
http://people-press.org/report/206/a-year-after-iraq-war
Ynet: One third of Palestinians (32%) supported the slaughter of a Jewish family, including the children:

http://pajamasmedia.com/tatler/2011/04/06/32-of-palestinians-support-infanticide/

http://www.ynetnews.com/articles/0,7340,L-4053251,00.html

World Public Opinion: 61% of Egyptians approve of attacks on Americans

32% of Indonesians approve of attacks on Americans

41% of Pakistanis approve of attacks on Americans

38% of Moroccans approve of attacks on Americans

83% of Palestinians approve of some or most groups that attack Americans (only 14% oppose)

62% of Jordanians approve of some or most groups that attack Americans (21% oppose)

42% of Turks approve of some or most groups that attack Americans (45% oppose)

A minority of Muslims disagreed entirely with terror attacks on Americans: (Egypt 34%; Indonesia 45%; Pakistan 33%)

About half of those opposed to attacking Americans were sympathetic with al-Qaeda's attitude toward the U.S.

http://www.worldpublicopinion.org/pipa/pdf/feb09/STARTII_Feb09_rpt.pdf

Pew Research (2010): 55% of Jordanians have a positive view of Hezbollah

30% of Egyptians have a positive view of Hezbollah

45% of Nigerian Muslims have a positive view of Hezbollah (26% negative)

43% of Indonesians have a positive view of Hezbollah (30% negative)

http://pewglobal.org/2010/12/02/muslims-around-the-world-divided-on-hamas-and-hezbollah/

Pew Research (2010): 60% of Jordanians have a positive view of Hamas (34% negative).

49% of Egyptians have a positive view of Hamas (48% negative)

49% of Nigerian Muslims have a positive view of Hamas (25% negative)

39% of Indonesians have a positive view of Hamas (33% negative)

http://pewglobal.org/2010/12/02/muslims-around-the-world-divided-on-hamas-and-hezbollah/

Pew Research (2010): 15% of Indonesians believe suicide bombings are often or sometimes justified.

34% of Nigerian Muslims believe suicide bombings are often or sometimes justified.

http://pewglobal.org/2010/12/02/muslims-around-the-world-divided-on-hamas-and-hezbollah/

Populus Poll (2006): 12% of young Muslims in Britain (and 12% overall) believe that suicide attacks against civilians in Britain can be justified. 1 in 4 support suicide attacks against British troops.

http://www.populuslimited.com/pdf/2006_02_07_times.pdf

http://www.danielpipes.org/blog/2005/07/more-survey-research-from-a-british-islamist

Pew Research (2007): 26% of younger Muslims in America believe suicide bombings are justified.

35% of young Muslims in Britain believe suicide bombings are justified (24% overall).

42% of young Muslims in France believe suicide bombings are justified (35% overall).

22% of young Muslims in Germany believe suicide bombings are justified.(13% overall).

29% of young Muslims in Spain believe suicide bombings are justified.(25% overall).

http://pewresearch.org/assets/pdf/muslim-americans.pdf#page=60

Pew Research (2011): 8% of Muslims in America believe suicide bombings are often or sometimes justified (81% never).

28% of Egyptian Muslims believe suicide bombings are often or sometimes justified (38% never).

http://www.people-press.org/2011/08/30/muslim-americans-no-signs-of-growth-in-alienation-or-support-for-extremism/

Pew Research (2007): Muslim-Americans who identify more strongly with their religion are three times more likely to feel that suicide bombings are justified

http://pewresearch.org/assets/pdf/muslim-americans.pdf#page=60

ICM: 5% of Muslims in Britain tell pollsters they would not report a planned Islamic terror attack to authorities.

27% do not support the deportation of Islamic extremists preaching violence and hate.

http://www.scotsman.com/?id=1956912005

http://www.danielpipes.org/blog/2005/07/more-survey-research-from-a-british-islamist.html

Federation of Student Islamic Societies: About 1 in 5 Muslim students in Britain (18%) would not report a fellow Muslim planning a terror attack.

http://www.fosis.org.uk/sac/FullReport.pdf

http://www.danielpipes.org/blog/2005/07/more-survey-research-from-a-british-islamist

ICM Poll: 25% of British Muslims disagree that a Muslim has an obligation to report terrorists to police.

http://www.icmresearch.co.uk/reviews/2004/Guardian%20Muslims%20Poll%20Nov%202004/Guardian%20Muslims%20Nov04.asp

http://www.danielpipes.org/blog/2005/07/more-survey-research-from-a-british-islamist

Populus Poll (2006): 16% of British Muslims believe suicide attacks against Israelis are justified.

37% believe Jews in Britain are a "legitimate target".

http://www.populuslimited.com/pdf/2006_02_07_times.pdf
http://www.danielpipes.org/blog/2005/07/more-survey-research-from-a-british-islamist
See also: http://wikiislam.net/wiki/Muslim_Statistics_(Terrorism) for further
statistics on Islamic terror. [93]

New York City Mayor Michael Bloomberg is a progressive whose infection with the virus has compromised his ability to discriminate and identify the sources of threat to the citizens of New York. Here is an example of Mayor Bloomberg's progressive distortion of reality. The bi-partisan 9/11 Commission report found that:

> "Mosques, schools, and boardinghouses served as recruiting stations in many parts of the world, including the United States..."A Muslim organization called al Khifa had numerous branch offices, the largest of which was in the Farouq mosque in Brooklyn. In the mid-1980s, it had been set up as one of the first outposts of Azzam and Bin Ladin's MAK. Other cities with branches of al Khifa included Atlanta, Boston, Chicago, Pittsburgh, and Tucson."

Brooklyn's Farouq mosque provided a safe haven and central command for the notorious blind Sheikh Omar Abel Rahman. It was at this mosque in Brooklyn that former Egyptian army officer, Ali Muhammed, helped to train Islamic jihadists.

---

[93] The Religion of Peace. Muslim Terrorist Polls, 2012.

Some of his students were convicted in the 1993 World Trade Center bombing, while other students of the Brooklyn mosque participated in the 1998 African embassy bombings.

On May 1, 2010, on a crowded Saturday night, a potentially horrific bomb was discovered in an abandoned SUV. Mayor Bloomberg gave an interview to another victim of the progressive virus, Katie Couric. Here is what the Mayor had to say:

> "If I had to guess 25 cents (he meant to say "bet")
> this would be something like that ... home-grown,
> maybe a mentally deranged person, someone with
> a political agenda, that doesn't like the healthcare
> bill or something. ... It could be anything."

The Mayor's opinions on the subject were in *total* disagreement with *every* forensic, police and FBI expert on the subject. Notice the divisive defaming of those who would oppose President Obama's Patient Protection and Affordable Care Act, by suggesting that those who disagreed with the President's health care plan were potentially mass murderers. Take note of the slight of hand that is characteristic of how progressives communicate. Mayor Bloomberg not only absolved those who are avowed enemies of the United States, but one and at the same time defamed Americans who would dare to disagree with a progressive-favored governmental policy. His kindred spirit,

Katie Couric, nodded approvingly and helped the Mayor with his choice of words in this progressive psychodrama designed to infect viewers with their cognitive distortions.

Everything about the Times Square crime scene was a spot-on, classic Islamic jihadist attack. Mayor Bloomberg's failure to either recognize or acknowledge this reality, while attempting to blame attempted mass murder on an opponent of a progressive boondoggle like ObamaCare, is a classic symptom of the progressive virus and it is dangerous to the citizens of New York.

As reported in *The New York Daily News*, the Times Square would-be mass murderer, Faisal Shahzad (see a pattern?), proudly said this in open court:

> "It's a war," Shahzad, 30, said in a hateful screed to Manhattan Federal Judge Miriam Cedarbaum. "I'm going to plead guilty a hundred times over because until the hour the U.S. pulls its forces from Iraq and Afghanistan and stops the drone strikes ... we will be attacking the U.S.," he said.
>
> "And I plead guilty to that."

We know now that this soldier of Islam was financed by Muslims in Yemen who targeted the citizens and visitors of New York City for mass murder. And he is not alone. The soldier of Islam who killed 13 Americans at Fort Hood, Major Nidal Malik

Hasan, prepared for his violent attack by changing his wardrobe from western wear into clothes typical of an Islamic jihadist martyr. As he fired approximately 100 rounds at American soldiers, ultimately killing 13, several witnesses reported that he shouted: "Allahu Akbar," or "God is great" in Arabic.

Despite this incontrovertible evidence of Hasan's mindset and classic Muslim jihadist modus operandi, apologists infected with the progressive virus in our native, vested media, have framed the Ft. Hood massacre as an example of "workplace violence." Progressives had to obviate the obvious because the virus infecting their mind demands that they not discriminate and identify differences in cultures and people on the dimension of threat.

Describing the Ft. Hood Jihad attack as an example of workplace violence is like characterizing a lethal shark attack as a drowning incident. I might add that Arabic news services have not framed either the Times Square bombing incident nor Major Hasan's murderous jihadist rage as anything but brave Muslim soldiers acting on behalf of traditional Islamic principles.

CHAPTER ELEVEN

The Progressive Virus in Action

The Financial Meltdown of 2008

IN 1994, PRESIDENT CLINTON directed HUD Secretary Henry Cisneros to come up with a plan to increase home ownership. Cisneros convened what HUD called a "historic meeting" of private and public housing-industry organizations in August of 1994. The group eventually produced a plan that incorporated creative measures to promote home ownership. The underlying motivation to increase home ownership was rooted in classic progressive dogma. That dogma asserts that all people, regardless of financial wherewithal, are *entitled* to own a home. The fact that people may not be able to afford to buy a home is, according to the cognitive distortions created by the progressive virus, nothing but one more example of social injustice. Cisneros, the Clintons and their minion were simply asserting a tried-and-true principle of progressivism when they concocted their housing scheme: Emphasis upon equal outcomes, NOT equal opportunity. Don't own a home? No problem, we'll (the government) take care of that.

Another die-hard progressive by the name of Congressman Barney Frank pressured Fannie Mae to make loans to people who would otherwise not qualify to buy a home, people who were destined to default on their loans. Frank pressured then Federal Reserve Chairman, Alan Greenspan, to lower interest rates to make it easier for the have-nots to qualify for a loan. Banks, under pressure from both the Clinton and Bush Administrations, were coerced into weakening home loan qualification criteria. Unfortunately, all of this progressive social engineering took place as the housing market bubble was reaching its "pop" point.

The extent to which progressives distort reality is stunning. In the mid-2000s, the looming housing bubble was denied to exist. During a House Financial Services Committee Hearing held on September 10, 2003, Congressman Frank, along with his fellow progressives on the committee, arrogantly dismissed the idea of a housing bubble and insolvency at Fannie Mae and Freddie Mac.

> Rep. Barney Frank (D., Mass.): "I worry, frankly, that there's a tension here. The more people, in my judgment, exaggerate a threat of safety and soundness, the more people conjure up the possibility of serious financial losses to the Treasury, which I do not see. I think we see

entities that are fundamentally sound financially and withstand some of the disaster scenarios. " [94]

When the committee reconvened on September 25, 2003, Frank had this to say:

> Rep. Frank: "I do think I do not want the same kind of focus on safety and soundness that we have in OCC [Office of the Comptroller of the Currency] and OTS [Office of Thrift Supervision]. I **want to roll the dice a little bit more in this situation towards subsidized housing.** "[95]
> (Emphasis added)

With reference to Congressman Frank's gambling analogy, the only problem with "rolling the dice" is that Mr. Frank was betting the taxpayer's money, not his.

One committee member not infected with the progressive virus predicted the disaster that was about to happen. It should go without saying that this committee member's prescient concerns were catalogued by the progressives on the committee as nothing more than an expression of social injustice.

> "Sen. Chuck Hagel (R., Neb.): Mr. Chairman, what we're dealing with is an astounding failure of

---

[94] House Financial Services Committee Hearing, Sept. 10, 2003.
[95] House Financial Services Committee Hearing, Sept. 25, 2003.

management and board responsibility, driven clearly by self interest and greed. And when we reference this issue in the context of – the best we can say is, "It's no Enron." Now, that's a hell of a high standard.

The very worst idea in the plan, which fortunately never gained approval, was to let first-time homebuyers freely tap their IRA and 401(k) retirement-savings plans with no penalty to scrounge up a down payment. That, HUD estimated, would have "benefited" 600,000 families in the first five years.

Plenty of other ideas in the plan did become reality, though. Knowing what we know now about the housing bust, the earnest language in the document seems faintly ridiculous. Here's an excerpt. Read it closely and you can see the seeds of disaster being planted:

For many potential homebuyers, the lack of cash available to accumulate the required down payment and closing costs is the major impediment to purchasing a home. Other households do not have sufficient available income to make the monthly payments on mortgages financed at market interest rates for standard loan terms. Financing strategies, fueled by the creativity and resources of the private and public sectors, should address both of these financial barriers to homeownership.

Note the praise for "creativity." That kind of creativity in stretching boundaries we could use less of. Mason puts it well: "It strikes me as reckless to promote home sales to individuals in such constrained financial predicaments." [96]

Wall Street bankers who are never at a loss to exploit a bad situation and feather their own nest, took these subsidized and fragile loans and packaged them into what investment bankers called "Collateralized Debt Obligations." (CDOs) Not only did the bankers package loans into a portfolio whose contents were a mystery to everyone, including the bankers who created them, they insured them through the likes of A.I.G. And just to make sure that unsuspecting "investors" had no fear about buying these CDOs, the bankers, their friends at the rating agencies, e.g., Standard and Poors and Moody's, gave these house of cards investments their highest rating.

The general population who had been thoroughly infected with the progressive virus lapped up the little or no money

---

[96] Bloomberg Businessweek. Bill Clinton's drive to increase home ownership went too far. Reported by Peter Coy. February 26, 2008 .

down loans with a sense of entitlement. Some mortgage companies were giving loans equal to 125% or even more of the home's inflated appraisal price. Americans infected with the progressive virus asked: Why should I not be able to buy a home just because I can't afford to buy it? It is said that a fool and his money soon part.

These nouveau pseudo rich who took advantage of the push toward equal outcomes included house "flippers" who would buy homes on credit with no down payment, slap a coat of cheap paint on and in it, then "flip" it within a couple of weeks for a net profit, sometimes as much as tens of thousands of dollars or more. Real Estate Agents were rolling in the dough. House salesmen leased Mercedes, BMWs and Lexus automobiles to drive their greed-frenzied-entitlement minded clients to the next open house. Dilapidated shacks near the California coast with less than 900 square feet on average size lots were going for over a million dollars, sometimes more.

An entire generation of entitled Americans thought of their home as their personal piggy bank. They sucked the money out of their over-inflated homes and used it to buy fancy cars, take grand vacations, buy luxury goods and live the lifestyle the progressive virus had convinced them they were entitled to have. This was all done on credit and none of the progressives in the government seemed concerned, that is, until the bubble burst in 2008.

Those who took out their easy loans defaulted on them with an equivalent easiness. Banks had so much red on their books that even they got scared. Their insurers were asked to underwrite so many bad loans that they, too, went bust. The collapse scared everyone and when all was said and done, it was the taxpayer who was coerced into bailing out those who, because of their progressive infection, raped and pillaged the American economy.

When those infected with the progressive virus emphasize equal outcomes over equal opportunity, they discount, if not completely destroy, the predicate behaviors that result in genuine success, like hard word, frugality, industry and patience. When banks mandated that those applying for a home mortgage had saved 20% of the down payment, while demonstrating a debt to income ratio that reflected an applicant who was responsible, they were protecting the money supply of the United States and rewarding hard work, industry and responsibility. Those infected with the progressive virus turned that working system on its head with an ill-conceived, ideologically driven, social engineering scheme that resulted in a financial debacle rivaling the great depression of the 1930s.

CHAPTER TWELVE

Asymmetrical Warfare

THE TERM ASYMMETRICAL WARFARE has traditionally been used to describe warfare between advanced nations and rag-tag guerilla militia groups or third world militaries. We use the term here to describe the asymmetrical warfare between progressive political leaders in the United States and their international adversaries. For illustration purposes we reference the communist state of North Korea, where even the cult of personality poses a formidable challenge to their progressive foes, and various theo-political states in the Middle-East.

Our primary focus will be upon the theo-political states and their militia sympathizers because they best illustrate the issues involved with asymmetrical warfare. The theo-political states we will focus on include Islamic theocracies intent upon establishing a new Caliphate, first in the Middle East, then expanding Sha'ria law to the rest of the world. In the simplest terms, the asymmetrical battle is characterized by a cold war between the believers versus the non-believers.

Progressives are, with few exceptions, comprised of agnostics or atheists. For those progressives who retain some semblance of spirituality, it is almost, without exception, a version of secular humanism. Progressive politicians know that they must shroud their agnosticism from a mostly Christian America and engage in a "for public consumption drama" of religious piousness. For every photo-op where Bill Clinton was seen entering a Christian church somewhere, when he was under stress who did he call? He called Anthony Robbins.

Progressives view theists in the same way they view quaint primitive tribes featured in a National Geographic documentary. Progressives tend to view Muslims as misguided fools who, if they only had access to money, education, sex and Western materialism, would "see the light."

Progressives are blinded by the psychological defense mechanism of projection when interacting with their theo-political adversaries. Progressives project their compass-less value system and narcissism upon people who are the exact opposite of them, in that they believe, have values (though arguably misguided values) and view Americans as devils who must be converted or eradicated.

Progressives are incapable of understanding that other people and cultures do not aspire to be like them. Progressive's insistence upon multiculturalism exacerbates this misunderstanding. Progressives are multicultural because they have no allegiance to any culture. This is due, in part, because as the virus mandates, all cultures and people *are* the same. Multiculturalism serves another important purpose for progressives. Multiculturalism helps to foment their revolutionary aspiration. It dissolves the connective tissue of traditional culture and, therefore, makes its victim country vulnerable to a progressive revolution.

A problem of major proportions arises when "other" cultures do not embrace multiculturalism. This is the rule, not the exception. In fact, not only do the vast majority of other cultures not embrace multiculturalism, they find it abhorrent.

Progressives are blinded to the fact that while they have no fixed values and no allegiance to the United States, other cultures and countries are rabidly jingoistic, nationalistic and view progressive's multiculturalism as an invitation to subordinate America. Most cultures are proudly incapable of assimilation. Some cultures consume and destroy American culture like a rapidly reproducing alien fish species that destroys the natural inhabitants of an American lake.

For example, in Muslim countries around the world, Muslim women are required to shroud their bodies to varying degrees lest they be punished by their husbands or by Sha'ria enforcers. Muslim men who immigrate to America bring with them their religious and political doctrines. To use a culinary analogy, Muslims may fold-in but they never mix. This means that their wives and female children must dress the way the Prophet Muhammad demanded.

Progressives don't understand this. They behave as though Islamic dress doctrine represent merely a style choice not a deep-rooted reflection of Islamic law. Progressive female journalists, for example, typically cloak themselves when around Muslim men or when visiting Islamic countries. I recall one financial journalist, somewhat famous for her feminist independence, traveling to a Middle-Eastern country and while there visited a clothing store where she was fitted for a burqa. How quaint and tolerant of her.

These progressive infected journalists behave as though they are merely changing their style of dress to suit or show respect to their hosts. But that is not what they are doing. *They are submitting to Islamic law and confirming to millions of Muslims that Islamic law is so powerful that even Western infidels submit to it.*

When it comes to the culture wars, progressives represent compass-less values and no allegiance to their native land. Deference to our adversaries by progressive political leaders exists everywhere, and is some places you would never expect it to exist.

Take for example NASA. NASA put a man on the moon in 1969. NASA has been responsible for some of the most impressive feats of science ever realized by mankind. So what do you think President Obama directed the head of NASA to make as one of his top priorities in 2010? Would you believe a mission to Mars? How about a new interstellar telescope? Why not focus on how to destroy the next asteroid that is targeting earth? No, none of these were made a priority. Before I tell you where the head of NASA was ordered to direct the administration's focus, on June 14, 2012 an asteroid the size of a city block nearly hit earth. LZ1, had it hit the earth, would have destroyed all life as we know it. What is troubling is that LZ1 was ONLY discovered on June 10, 2012, four days before its near miss! One might reason that NASA should be encouraged to focus on such threats, yes?

> In a July 2, 2010 interview with Al Jazeera, Charles Bolden, head of NASA, told Imran Garda that when he took over at NASA, President Obama had directed him to "find a way to reach out to the Muslim world and engage much more with dominantly Muslim nations to help them feel good about their historic contribution to science and math and engineering." [97]

---

[97] Al Jazeera. July 2, 2010 Interview with NASA Chief, Charles Bolden.

Should we be comforted that although earth remains vulnerable to a cataclysmic asteroid strike our Muslim brethren have been made to "feel good" about themselves by the social engineers at the White House? Progressives believe their feel good, progressive-speak is a language universally accepted. In fact, such behavior is seen as a crystal clear example of vulnerability and weakness. Muslim countries viewed Mr. Obama's NASA overture to them as acknowledgement of their rightful place in the world of science right along with the United States.

North Korea has a long history of breaking every single agreement forged with the United States. What is the response from our progressive leaders? Progressive-speak that sounds remarkably like what progressive parents say to their children when they do something their parents don't want them to do: "You need a timeout." "No more access to your iPhone or iPad for a week." The pattern found in this example of asymmetrical warfare would be laughable if it were not so serious.

Progressive leaders labor under the delusional belief that progressive America can be bottled up and either given or imposed on Muslim countries. Not only does Islam find progressives and their ideology an abomination, but while Islam finds progressive's attempts to subvert Islam an abomination, Islam is busy doing what it has always done, expand its universe of influence. Islam has its eyes on America. Likewise, North

Korea is intent upon developing technology that will permit it to threaten the west coast of the United States with a nuclear-tipped intercontinental ballistic missile. What "timeout" progressive-speak is appropriate for a country like North Korea whose citizens have never laid eyes on an iPhone or iPad?

Islam is both a religion and an imperialist political movement. Islam's entire history has been one of conquering its enemies in the name of Allah. No enemies are more devilish than the twin devils of the United States and Israel.

The modus operandi of the 9/11 perpetrators, like their fathers and their fathers before them, can be catalogued as a two-stage operation. The first stage of this virulent pattern involves the destruction or commandeering of an iconic edifice located within the borders of a perceived enemy of Islam. The second stage of this assaultive pattern of conduct is for Islamic financiers to back the construction of a mosque at or near the ruins of their enemy's monument or edifice.

Rather than planting a flag or simply leaving the "infidel's" edifices in ruins, Islamic jihadist's mark their enemy's territory with a brick and mortar edifice in the form of an Islamic mosque. This pattern consistently finds that the choice of location for these displays of dominance and victory is solely determined by the location of the destroyed or commandeered structures of their enemy.

Marking one's adversary's territory cuts across all cultures and even includes the animal kingdom where marking the territory of a competitor is recognized as a reliable indicator of an impending attempt to confiscate the territory of another. In the animal kingdom marking is accomplished by the depositing of bodily fluids and secretions upon the competitor's territory.

Among humans, entry level marking may take the form of the placement of symbols, e.g., graffiti, flags, etc. Intrusive markings are almost always achieved by the construction of an edifice within the geographical borders of another's territory.

In order to distinguish innocent intrusion or the free expression of cultural markings into another's cultural or geographical turf, from a marking that is imperialistic in nature, one need only determine whether or not the act of marking another's territory occurs concurrently with the jealous protection or outright prohibition of marking by others. Islam meets the criteria for designation as an imperialistic marker in that it has and continues to engage in the systematic marking of non-Muslim countries with their mosques and the push for Sha'ria courts while outlawing even minimal displays of non-Muslim religious or progressive symbols within their defined territories.

To illustrate, in July of 2000, the Saudi Ministry of Legal Endowments set forth an enforceable edict on the building of

Christian churches and Jewish temples, among other "heresy" religions in Muslim countries. The fatwa, in full force as of the writing of this book, reads as follows:

"The Permanent Council for Scholarly Research and Religious Legal Judgment has studied the queries some individuals brought before the Chief Mufti… concerning the topic of the construction of houses of worship for unbelievers in the Arabian Peninsula, such as the construction of churches for Christians and houses of worship for Jews and for other unbelievers and [the question of] the owners of companies or organizations allotting a fixed place for their unbelieving workers to perform the rites of unbelief.

After considering the queries the Council answered as follows:

All religions other than Islam are heresy and error. Any place designated for worship other than [that of] Islam is a place of heresy and error, for it is forbidden to worship Allah in any way other than the way that Allah has prescribed in Islam. The law of Islam (Sha'ria) is the final and definitive religious law. It applies to all men and jinns and abrogates all that came before it. This is a matter about which there is consensus. (Emphasis added)

Those who claim that there is truth in what the Jews say, or in what the Christians say – whether he is one of them or not – is denying the Koran and the Prophet Muhammad's sunna and the consensus of the Muslim nation... Allah said: 'The only reason I sent you was to bring good tidings and warnings to all [Koran 34:28]'; 'Oh people, I am Allah's Messenger to you all [Koran 7:158]'; 'Allah's religion is Islam [3:19]'; 'Whoever seeks a religion other than Islam, it shall not be accepted from him [3:85]'; 'The unbelievers from among the people of the Book [i.e. Jews and Christians] and the polytheists are in hellfire and will be [there] forever. They are the worst of all creation... [98:6].'

Therefore, religion necessitates the prohibition of unbelief, and this requires the prohibition of worshiping Allah in any way other than that of the Islamic Sha'ria. Included in this is the prohibition against building houses of worship according to the abrogated religious laws, Jewish or Christian or anything else, since these houses of worship — whether they be churches or other houses of worship — are considered heretical houses of worship, because the worship that is practiced in them is in violation of the Islamic Sha'ria, which abrogates all religious law that came before it. Allah says about the unbelievers and their deeds: 'I will turn to every deed they have done and I will make them into dust in the wind [Koran 25:23].' [98]

Progressive leaders have conflated the political and legal system that is Islam with their ethnocentric understanding of what constitutes a religion. Progressive's view of religion is skewed by their devout agnosticism or abject atheism.

Progressive's skewed understanding of Christianity, for example, makes it virtually impossible for them to grasp the intent and motivations of Muslims. The avowed ideals of tolerance, truth and peace, found within all sects of Christianity and Judaism, are erroneously assumed to be a part of Islam, because after all, Islam is a religion as well. Progressives equate

---

[98] Saudi Ministry of Legal Endowments An enforceable edict on the building of Christian churches and Jewish temples, among other "heresy" religions in Muslim countries. July, 2000.

Christianity with Islam and erroneously conclude that both religions are comprised of "radicals" and "moderates."

The political and legal DNA of Islam cannot be separated from the religious component of Islam because they are one in the same. Islam is dedicated, by edict, to the annihilation of non-Islamic political and legal systems. Muhammad commands the imposition of Sha'ria law upon all non-Muslim countries by the use of force, if necessary. That command is non-negotiable and is not open to interpretation.

Those infected with the progressive virus erroneously believe that the Qur'an is open to interpretation, like any other religious text because progressives believe that the Qur'an was written, in a style approximating the Bible or Torah, using metaphors, parables and stories open to interpretation. Progressives commit a classic ethnocentric error by projecting their assumptions about what they consider religious thought onto the edicts of Islam. Thus, progressives believe there to be moderate Muslims and radical Muslims, when no such distinction can be found in any interpretation of the Qur'an because the Qur'an is comprised of crystal clear commands that do not easily lend themselves to personal interpretation. Although theologians can and do make distinctions between Christianity and Islam, progressives do not make such distinctions. Their mandated cognitive distortion of convenient equilibrium creates sameness between all religions. Moreover, progressives view Islam, Christianity and Judaism from an atheist's sensibility. "It is all crazy myth," according to Western progressives. Despite progressive's lumping distortions, real differences do exist.

Unlike the Christian Bible, for example, that was authored by multiple writers spanning hundreds of years using metaphors, parables and stories that address various moral and ethical issues, the Qur'an is a book containing **precisely written commands authored by one person during his lifetime, the Prophet Muhammad.**

Inconsistencies among commands found in the Qur'an are resolved unlike any other religious text. The Qur'an specifically notes that where any command may be open to differing interpretations, **the later command supersedes any other command written at an earlier time.** The commands in the Qu'ran, supporting peace and tolerance, have been clearly superseded by commands imploring violence, intolerance and strict punishment for non-believers. The Prophet Muhammad was a brilliant military leader and tactician, after all.

Multiculturalism is an abomination in Islam, as is homosexuality, equality between the sexes, the American civil and criminal justice system. Western dress, most music and most art have been targeted for annihilation by command of the

Prophet himself, Muhammad. Imagine how Muslims feel when they see female and male American soldiers on their soil?

Islam's territorial marking serves to announce the first step toward the imposition of Sha'ria law. As noted earlier, Islamic imperialism is characterized by a two-staged operation, with the first stage often preceding the final stage by years or even decades. The first stage involves the identification of an iconic structure within its perceived enemy's territory. Once identified, this structure is either commandeered or destroyed. The second stage involves the construction of a brick and mortar edifice that "marks" the now commandeered or destroyed area. The edifice that is virtually always chosen as the "marking agent" is the Islamic mosque.

Islamic imperialism is distinct from Western imperialism. Traditionally, Western imperialism has been cynically viewed as an attempt to expand capitalist markets. Such is not the case with Islam. Islam commands that the infidels of the world be converted to Islam. This conversion includes conversion by force, if necessary. Thus, Islamic imperialism is a theo-political not an economically motivated ambition.

Islamic imperialism has a long history. To illustrate, Muhammad identified, then destroyed, an iconic pantheon known to all the citizens of Mecca, named the Ka'aba. The identification of this structure preceded his invasion of Mecca that took place in 630 CE. Once in control of the city, the prophet ordered that this iconic structure be rebuilt as an Islamic mosque. Muhammad left Mecca and onto other conquests, but not before constructing a brick and mortar message to the citizens of Mecca that Islam had arrived along with the imposition of Sha'ria law.

In yet another example of this two-staged assault on non-Muslim countries, Muslim soldiers, led by Caliph Umar, laid the foundation of the Al-Aqsa mosque on the Temple Mount. This location, like the twin towers, was chosen for marking because of its richly symbolic meaning to the perceived enemy of Islam, people of the Jewish faith.

The iconic Church of St. John, located in Damascus, was commandeered by Muslim soldiers in a bloody battle that took place in the year 705. Muslim financiers then paid for the transformation of this symbol of Christianity into the Ummayad Victory Mosque.

Ottoman Sultan Mehmet conquered Constantinople in 1453. He targeted the Hagia Sophia, the towering building that represented the home of Orthodox Christianity, for marking. In front of what was then the largest church in the world, the sultan bowed down, sprinkled soil on his turban and said: "There is no God but God, and Muhammad is his prophet."

This pattern repeated itself in India at the site of over 2000 Hindu temples, most notably the temple that commemorated the birthplace of Lord Rama, located in Ayhodhya. This Hindu temple had survived for hundreds of years until 1528. When the Muslim Mughals invaded India, true to their two-staged marking modus operandi, they targeted the Lord Rama temple for destruction. They marked the Hindu's territory with the Babri mosque. The Babri mosque stood as an Islamic victory mosque until 1992 when it was re-marked and re-claimed by Hindus.

Between 1941 and 1945, Muslim Croats targeted the iconic structure known as the Artists Gallery Museum for marking. With funding from Muslim financiers, they refashioned the museum with minarets and converted it into an Islamic mosque. In 1974, when the Muslim Turks invaded Cyprus, numerous Orthodox churches in the northern part of the country were either razed or commandeered, then converted into "reminder" mosques. The systematic marking one's enemy's territory as a preamble to the forced imposition of Sha'ria law continues to this day.

This brings us to the proposed building of a mosque at Ground Zero. Progressives, true to their cognitive distortions and need to eradicate Judeo-Christian values, framed the Ground Zero Mosque as a "freedom of religion" issue. This is ironic because progressives are agnostic or atheist. In reality, the construction of the Ground Zero Mosque was consistent with their multicultural edict and their need to eradicate Western religious influence.

Permit me to address the forensic meaning of naming the proposed mosque near Ground Zero the "Cordoba Mosque." The name "Cordoba" is a transparent reference, rising to the level of a "slap in your face" homage, to the Cordoba Mosque that was built near the site of the iconic Spanish Christian church that was, just like the World Trade Center Towers, destroyed by Muslim jihadists and martyrs.

The choice of where to build victory mosques in non Islamic countries has always been determined by where best to send a message of Islamic supremacy to not only the vanquished but those within Islam who would dare to challenge this assaultive and imperialistic pattern of conduct.

The driving force behind the "Cordoba" mosque, Imam Feisal Abdul Rauf, has promised that it will be a Sha'ria compliant mosque. In his book: *Islam: A Sacred Law – What Every Muslim Should Know About Sha'ria* [99], he extols and promotes the Wahhabi and Salafi doctrines, the exact same doctrines used as blueprints for the Muslim guerilla soldiers who attacked New York City in 1993, 2001 and 2010. Apologists and supporters of the Ground Zero mosque confuse the edifice

---

[99] Sha'ria in Arabic: ريعـة

with a house of worship as opposed to a symbol that serves the dual purpose of marking the enemy's territory but an edifice that also serves as a peripheral military command cell that relies upon its misidentification as a religious edifice to protect it from detection.

Other nations under assault have come to recognize the clear and present danger that many mosques represent. The al Quds mosque, located in Hamburg, Germany, served as a launching pad and training ground for the leaders of the 9/11 attack upon New York City. In early September 2010, the German government shut down the al Quds mosque. "We have closed the mosque because it was a recruiting and meeting point for Islamic radicals who wanted to participate in so-called jihad or holy war," said Frank Reschreiter, a spokesman for the Hamburg state interior ministry.

Closer to home, Brooklyn's Farouq mosque provided a safe haven and central command for the notorious blind Sheikh Omar Abel Rahman. It was at this mosque in Brooklyn that former Egyptian army officer, Ali Muhammed, helped to train Islamic jihadists. Some of his students were convicted in the 1993 World Trade Center bombing, while other students of the Brooklyn mosque participated in the 1998 African embassy bombings.

A plan is afoot to commandeer the Tomb of the Patriarchs and the Tomb of Rachel, iconic holy sites to Jews everywhere. Consistent with the pattern outlined herein, these Judaic holy sites have been targeted for "re-designation" into Islamic mosques, using the political arm of The United Nations Educational, Scientific and Cultural Organization. (UNESCO) Mosques, with reference to their status as a "safe" zone, where terrorist plots and plotters are off limits to their intended victims, represent a difference in kind when compared to both Christian churches and Jewish Temples.

American-born Imam Anwar Awlaki preached at the Rabat mosque in San Diego where he networked with some of the 9/11 conspirators. Some moved to Northern Virginia at the same time Awlaki did, where they set up camp at the Dar al Hijra mosque. One of Awlaki's best students was none other than Major Nidal Malick Hasan who, as we know, massacred 13 Americans at Fort Hood. Awlaki used Yemeni mosques as his staging centers and headquarters. Recall it was Muslim financiers from Yemen who backed the failed Times Square bomber, Faisal Shahzad.

While America is helping to fund the so-called Arab Spring, Islam has its eyes on subordinating America and the rest of Europe to Sha'ria law. Islam has an inherent advantage in this asymmetrical war because it is comprised of citizens who are not plagued with the progressive virus. This means that they can focus, stay tuned-in and will stay true to their values. By naming anti-American, anti-West Islamic revolutions "The Arab Spring," Western progressives have proven themselves to be incapable of perceiving deadly threats to America. Their cognitive distortions border on delusional.

Progressives view all religions as functionally the same mythology, with a few twists and turns unique to the culture that generated it. This skewing of reality derives from the progressive virus's tendency to create in its victim narcissism and the unquestioned, self-evident dogma that man creates reality and values. Nothing could be further from the truth.

The Qur'an mandates, in no uncertain terms, that Muslims must impose Sha'ria law on all non-Muslims, that is, if they cannot first be converted. Sha'ria is a specific set of laws, a legal system that deals with both civil and criminal matters and is as specific as Westerner's civil and criminal justice system. Sha'ria law covers ritual worship, transactions, contracts, morals, manners, beliefs and punishments. The Qur'an makes it crystal clear that "man-made" governments, e.g., democracy and documents like the Bill of Rights, are abominations and must be eliminated.

The term "Creeping Sha'ria" is a specific term understood by Muslims to be the method by which non-Muslim countries are converted to Sha'ria law. Step-by-step, virtually unnoticeable inroads or creeping is the path to eventually taking over the world. Remarkably, the United Kingdom already has Sha'ria courts that supercede British law. Germany, Sweden, Belgium and the United States are already experiencing the push to institute Sha'ria courts. In recognition of the push to impose Sha'ria law, legislatures all over the United States are enacting laws designed to prevent Creeping Sha'ria. It will come as no surprise that progressive politicians are against these laws. Muslims persist in their quest to impose Sha'ria law, for example:

"After heated debates in two dozen states over banning Sha'ria law, the legal code of Islam, a national Islamic group is beginning a multi-million dollar effort to explain how Sha'ria applies to the lives of American Muslims.

"The Islamic Circle of North America, a New York-based group, is spending $3 million on its Defending Religious Freedom campaign, which kicks off Monday (March, 2012) and explains Sha'ria law and common misunderstandings.

The effort includes billboards, TV and radio ads in 25 major cities, including New York, Los Angeles and Chicago, in addition to town hall meetings and seminars on university campuses led by Muslim academics and activists. Each directs audiences to a website and manned hotline, 1-855-Shariah.

The campaign is a response to efforts to ban Sha'ria law over the last two years in state legislatures and on ballot initiatives, said Naeem Baig, vice president of public affairs for Islamic Circle of North America. Republican presidential candidates also have raised the Sharia debate.

Tennessee, Louisiana and Arizona have passed laws banning judges from consulting Sha'ria, or more generally, foreign or religious laws. Oklahoma voters approved a ban on Sharia law in 2010, but a judge blocked the rule after a Muslim man filed a religious freedom lawsuit. Legislatures in South Carolina and Florida are considering anti-Sha'ria bills.

'It's a small minority of Islamophobes that are pushing the anti-Sha'ria bills, but it's becoming mainstream. Now, even presidential hopefuls like Newt Gingrich and Rick Santorum are talking about Sharia,' said Baig. We see it not only an issue of Sha'ria but an issue of broader religious freedom.

Sha'ria law attacks come mostly from those fearing radical Muslims are introducing extreme interpretations of Islamic law, such as those practiced in Afghanistan under the Taliban, into American society." [100]

This article is very telling in that not only does it reveal that the push to impose Sha'ria law if alive and well in the United States, but that apologists for Islam have mastered the progressive's PC Scarlet Letter ruse (Islamophobe) to mark those who would dare to expose Muslim's imperialistic motivations and to challenge the myth of the "moderate" versus "radical" Muslim. Ironically, it is an abiding respect for Islam, and its influence as a potent theo-political force, that is missing once filtered through the cognitive distortions of the progressive virus.

---

[100] Huffington Post. Religion. Sha'ria Law Campaign Begins As Muslim Group Fights Bans. By: Jaweed Kaleem. March 12, 2012.

Specific examples of Sha'ria law, not open to interpretation, include that drinkers and gamblers may be whipped, permits husbands to hit their wives (plural). Sha'ria allows for an injured plaintiff to exact revenge in the form of an "eye for an eye." A thief may, but not necessarily, have his hand cut off. Sha'ria demands that homosexuals or homosexual behavior be punished by death, usually by beheading or hanging. Sha'ria orders that "fornicators" be whipped and adulterers (usually women) be stoned until they are dead. It commands the punishment of death to both Muslim and non-Muslims who criticize Muhammad, The Qur'an or Sha'ria law. Sha'ria commands that a defector from Islam be killed. Sha'ria commands aggressive, unjust and violent Jihad.

Sha'ria courts handle issues related to divorce, domestic violence and financial disputes. No separation of "church and state" exists even in its most nascent form in Islamic countries. The religious component of Islam cannot be separated from the political force that it represents. This is why Muslim countries are, virtually without exception, outright theocracies or aspiring to be full-fledged theocracies. The so-called "Arab Spring" can be operationally defined as the effort to impose theocratic rule in Muslim countries. Why would America finance and offer moral support for this transformation? The answer can be found in progressive's cognitive distortions.

A classic example of how progressives are incapable of processing information accurately, we cite to comedienne and social commentator Rosie O'Donnell's equating of "radical" Christianity with "radical" Islam. Rosie O'Donnell said this in September of 2006:

> "Radical Christianity is just as threatening as radical Islam in a country like America". [101]

Ms. O'Donnell is not alone in her opinion, her views reflect progressives everywhere. Here is the truth on the subject without the distortions of the progressive virus.

> The death penalty is currently the punishment for being homosexual or engaging in homosexual behavior in Saudi Arabia, Iran, Mauritania, northern Nigeria, Sudan, and Yemen. [102] [103] Homosexuality formerly carried the death penalty in Afghanistan under the Taliban, but has since changed from a capital crime to one that is punished with fines and a prison sentence. When America and its allies leave Afghanistan, we anticipate that the death penalty will be reinstated.

Ms. O'Donnell should realize that the countries listed above are populated by and governed by mainstream Muslims, not

---

[101] ABC Television. *The View*. Rosie O'Donnell. September 12, 2006.

[102] Homosexuality and Islam". Religion Facts. 2005-07-19.

[103] 7 countries still put people to death for same-sex acts". ILGA.

"radical" Muslims. Mainstream, middle-of-the-road Islam is vehemently anti-homosexual, period. This anti-homosexual edict is so powerful that homosexuality, as a behavior, is denied to exist by some Muslim leaders. For example, in September of 2007 the President of Iran, Mahmoud Ahmadinejad, addressed the issue homosexuality:

> "In Iran we don't have homosexuals like in your country," Iranian President Mahmoud Ahmadinejad said at Columbia University last night in response to a question about the recent execution of two gay men there. "In Iran we do not have this phenomenon," he continued. "I do not know who has told you we have it." [104]

> "In the Muslim countries of Bahrain, Qatar, Algeria, Uzbekistan and the Maldives, homosexuality is punished with jail time, fines or corporal punishment. In Saudi Arabia, while the maximum punishment for homosexual acts is public execution, the government will generally use lesser punishments, e.g., fines, jail time, and whipping—as alternatives, unless it feels that

---

[104] U.K.'s Mail Online. September 25, 2007.

individuals are challenging state authority by engaging in LGBT social movements." [105]

In other words, Ms. O'Donnell, you will be spared public execution if you do NOT engage in advocating on behalf of LGBT causes and issues. Are you engaged in LGBT social movements Ms. O'Donnell?

"Iran is the nation that executes the largest number of its citizens for homosexual acts. Since the 1979 Islamic revolution, the Iranian government has executed more than 4,000 such people. In Egypt, openly gay men have been prosecuted under general public morality laws. On the other hand, homosexuality, while not legal, is tolerated to some extent in Lebanon." [106]

Muslims must find it a gift from Allah that their enemies, like Ms. O'Donnell and her progressive cohorts, are so deluded and, therefore, vulnerable.

One of the more effective tactics Muslims use to subvert their enemies is called: Taqiyya (TA-KEE-YAH). [107] Muslims are permitted, in fact are encouraged, to deceive non-Muslims, if it advances the cause of Islam. Progressives are so deluded by

---

[105] Is Beheading Really the Punishment for Homosexuality in Saudi Arabia?" Sodomylaws.org.
[106] Ibid.
[107] In Arabic: ﯨـﻘ

their compass-less values that Muslims applying Taqiyya techniques find it embarrassingly easy to deceive the West's progressive leaders. While progressives project their delusions onto other cultures, Muslims are instructed to lie to non-Muslims about their beliefs, their political ambitions and their imperialistic agenda.

Taqiyya should be easy to understand because progressives, like their Muslim brethren, adhere to the end justifies the means social interaction principle. We see Taqiyya illustrated when Muslim leaders say one thing to the Western press then say the polar opposite for Arabic media. For example, The Islamic American Relief Agency (IARA) (refer back to how progressives give their organizations non-threatening names) collected hundreds of thousands of dollars for orphans. In reality, The IARA gave the money to Jihadists intent upon terrorizing non-Muslim infidels. The Muslim press knew about the true intent of IARA, but gullible Americans and their progressive infected press did not. More subtle examples of Taqiyya deserve attention.

For example, Westerners have heard that Islam is a "religion of peace," and to prove that Muslims will quote from the earlier, more peaceful part of the Qur'an, as an act of Taqiyya. They do this knowing full well that the command they are quoting to create the impression of peacefulness has been abrogated. This is because it preceded a later command, made by the Prophet Muhammad. The fact is, the Qur'an declares that the ONLY way for there to be peace in the world is when each and every country in the world is converted to Islam and Sha'ria law.

Progressives cannot grasp the power of Islam, and therefore, cannot grasp the power and dedication of Muslims to their beliefs. This is because progressives believe that like any religious group of people, Muslims are misguided because they have faith and they must be, by definition, uneducated. Such is not the case.

Muslim jihadists are well educated, smart and know what they are doing. Unlike America's schizophrenic mass shooters, Muslim jihadists are perfectly cogent in their thoughts and ideas. The following study addresses this issue. The Islamic author examining this subject began with this quote:

> You have trivialized our movement by
> your mundane analysis. May God have
> mercy on you...Ayman al-Zawahiri.

> "We find that graduates from subjects such as science, engineering, and medicine are strongly overrepresented among Islamist movements in the Muslim world, though not among the extremist Islamic groups which have emerged in

Western countries more recently. We also find that engineers alone are strongly over-represented among graduates in violent groups in both realms. This is all the more puzzling for engineers are virtually absent from left-wing violent extremists and only present rather than over-represented among right-wing extremists. We consider four hypotheses that could explain this pattern. Is the engineers' prominence among violent Islamists an accident of history amplified through network links, or do their technical skills make them attractive recruits? Do engineers have a 'mindset' that makes them a particularly good match for Islamism, or is their vigorous radicalization explained by the social conditions they endured in Islamic countries? We argue that the interaction between the last two causes is the most plausible explanation of our findings, casting a new light on the sources of Islamic extremism and grounding macro theories of radicalization in a micro-level perspective." [108]

---

[108] Gambetta, Diego, Hertog Steffen. *Engineers of Jihad*. University of Oxford Sociology Working Papers. Paper Number 2007-10.

The "mundane analysis" quote by Ayman al-Zawahiri is a direct reference to one of the key characteristics of asymmetrical warfare when on one side you find valueless, compass-less, narcissistic progressive political leaders in a battle with true believers who are willing to give their life in support of their religion and political aspirations. One of the wealthiest men in the world, the late Osama bin Laden, gave up many of the material spoils progressive life had to offer to pursue his jihad against America and the West. Name one progressive multi-billionaire who would do the same.

Islam should not be trivialized nor should it be misunderstood as a passing phenomenon. The realities of biology and reproductive rates are on Islam's side. While progressive women were busy arrogantly declaring that they would never reproduce due to the Earth's over population and its effect on the environment, Muslims were and are busy having lots of children and passing their religion and their genes onto their offspring. Progressives have all but ignored biology because to affirm their tabula rasa dogma they must negate biology. Again, Muslims must find their enemy's delusional mindset as a supportive sign from Allah.

CNN did a study of the top 4,500 names given to newborns in Great Britain in 2010. Mohammed was the top choice, with Oliver coming in second. Mohammed was the most popular boy's name in the four largest Dutch cities in 2009. The Pew Research Center published these data in 2011:

"The world's Muslim population is expected to increase by about 35% in the next 20 years, rising from 1.6 billion in 2010 to 2.2 billion by 2030, according to new population projections by the Pew Research Center's Forum on Religion & Public Life.

Globally, the *Muslim population is forecast to grow at about twice the rate of the non-Muslim population over the next two decades –* an average annual growth rate of 1.5% for Muslims, compared with 0.7% for non-Muslims. If current trends continue, Muslims will make up 26.4% of the world's total projected population of 8.3 billion in 2030, up from 23.4% of the estimated 2010 world population of 6.9 billion.

While the global Muslim population is expected to grow at a faster rate than the non-Muslim population, the Muslim population nevertheless is expected to grow at a slower pace in the next two decades than it did in the previous two decades. From 1990 to 2010, the global Muslim population increased at an average annual rate of 2.2%, compared with the projected rate of 1.5% for the period from 2010 to 2030.

In the United States, for example, the population projections show the number of Muslims more than doubling over the next two decades, rising from 2.6 million in 2010 to 6.2 million in 2030, in large part because of immigration and higher-than-average fertility among Muslims. The Muslim share of the U.S. population (adults and children) is projected to grow from 0.8% in 2010 to 1.7% in 2030, making Muslims roughly as numerous as Jews or Episcopalians are in the United States today. Although several European countries will have substantially higher percentages of Muslims, the United States is projected to have a larger number of Muslims by 2030 than any European country other than Russia and France. [109]

---

[109] Pew Research Center. The Future of the Global Muslim Population. Projections for 2010-2030. January 27, 2011.

The London Telegraph addressed this issue in 2009 with this headline:

Muslim Europe: the demographic time bomb transforming our continent. The EU is facing an era of vast social change, reports Adrian Michaels, and few politicians are taking notice

The article went on to present these facts:

"Europe's low white birth rate, coupled with faster multiplying migrants, will change fundamentally what we take to mean by European culture and society. Britain and the rest of the European Union are ignoring a demographic time bomb: a recent rush into the EU by migrants, including millions of Muslims, will change the continent beyond recognition over the next two decades, and almost no policy-makers are talking about it. The numbers are startling. Only 3.2 per cent of Spain's population was foreign-born in 1998. In 2007 it was 13.4 per cent. Europe's Muslim population has more than doubled in the past 30 years and will have doubled again by 2015. In Brussels, the top seven baby boys' names recently were Mohamed, Adam, Rayan, Ayoub, Mehdi, Amine and Hamza. Europe's low white birth rate, coupled with faster multiplying migrants, will change fundamentally what we take to mean by European culture and society. The altered population mix has far-reaching implications for education, housing, welfare, labour, the arts and everything in between...[W]hites will be in a minority in Birmingham by 2026, says Christopher Caldwell, an American journalist, and even sooner in Leicester. Another forecast holds that Muslims could outnumber non-Muslims in France and perhaps in all of western Europe by mid-century. Austria was 90 per cent Catholic in the 20th century but Islam could be the majority religion among Austrians aged under 15 by 2050, says Mr Caldwell. " [110]

In 2005 a meeting took place in Chicago, Illinois. It was comprised of 24 Islamic organizations. Those organizations planned out their strategy to change America into an Islamic country using journalists, education, the media and politics, that is, those infected with the progressive virus. Here is what they said:

---

[110] London Telegraph. Muslim Europe: the demographic time bomb transforming our continent. By Adrian Michaels. Aug 2009.

"We must prepare ourselves for the reality that in 50 years there will be 50 million Muslims living in America." [111]

Muammar Al Gaddafi said this before his death:

"We don't need terrorists, we don't need bombers, the 50 million-plus Muslims in Europe will turn it into a Muslim continent within a few decades." [112]

The realities of asymmetrical warfare between progressives and Islam are tilted in Islam's favor. Progressives are blind to the realities confronting them at every turn. They label people who would dare to scientifically analyze demographic trends and who would give respect to Islam as a powerful imperialistic political force as Islamophobes. Their labels betray their blindness to the strengths and power of true believers, who compete with compass-less narcissists infected with the progressive virus. When reality is competing with you in a winner take all match, and you don't even know it because you think that you create reality, your adversary will overwhelm you. It is only a matter of time, or as progressive's enemies would say: إن شـــاء الله [113]

---

[111] Islamic Strategy Conference. Chicago, Illinois. 2005.

[112] Al Jazeera TV, Broadcast in Qatar. April 10, 2006.

[113] Arabic for: God Willing.

CHAPTER THIRTEEN

The Hollywood Elite and the Progressive Virus

CERTAIN DEMOGRAPHIC GROUPS ARE particularly susceptible to the progressive virus. One group that deserves our attention is made up of the so-called Hollywood elite.

Recall that Descartes asserted "Je pense donc je suis"; (I think, therefore I am) and that Sartre believed that he could become anything he imagined. This reminds me of a rather well known book on acting entitled: *Acting is Believing.*

A key component of the progressive virus is that it convinces its victim that he or she can become anything or anyone by adopting a role or thinking it. Recall that being wealthy removes natural immune system barriers and makes it easier for the virus to commandeer the machinery of the mind. Add to that recipe the fact that mind-altering substances exacerbate the infection with the progressive virus. Look closely and you will see that the lives of Hollywood's elite constitute the perfect medium within which the progressive virus can flourish.

Southern California, especially the Westside and Hollywood in Los Angeles County, are hot spots for posh-progressives who spout and promote progressive dogma using their presentation talent and financial wherewithal to infect others. Challenge progressive dogma and you can expect to be attacked first, and perhaps most viciously, by the Hollywood elite.

Ben Shapiro has researched Hollywood's elite. Shapiro, a Harvard trained lawyer, and author of *Primetime Propaganda: The True Hollywood Story of How the Left Took Over Your TV*, studied how the Hollywood progressive colony is dedicated to infecting the public when they consume media the elite produce, direct, write and act in.

Shapiro interviewed more than one hundred of the industry's biggest players, including Larry Gelbart (M*A*S*H), Fred Silverman (former president of ABC Entertainment, NBC, and vice president of programming at CBS), Marta Kauffman (Friends), David Shore (House), and Mark Burnett (Survivor). Many of these insiders boast that not only is Hollywood biased against conservatives, but that many of the shows being broadcast have secret or subliminal political messages. One thing Shapiro clearly demonstrated is that Hollywood is a "closed shop." Those not infected with the progressive virus, that is, conservatives, are persona non grata and need not apply.

"Friends creator Marta Kauffman acknowledged
that she consciously put together a writing staff

"of mostly liberal people." When asked if conservatives are discriminated against in Hollywood, writer-director Nicholas Meyer responded: "Well, I hope so." When Shapiro interviewed Laugh-In creator George Schlatter, he was treated to a lengthy diatribe about the "balloon buffoon" Rush Limbaugh and Ann Coulter, whom he said represented: "one of the main reasons we should legalize abortion but make it retroactive." [114]

In a particularly brilliant study on the subject of Hollywood and its political inclinations, Clemson professors Todd D. Kendall and John E. Walker conducted research entitled: *An Empirical Analysis of Political Activity in Hollywood.* In their abstract they wrote this:

> "Film plays an important role in the American political system, and forms an important branch of the mass media. I analyzed the political contributions of a sample of 996 top film actors, directors, producers and writers, correlating them with demographic, family, and career success variables. I find that contributions flow overwhelmingly to left-of-center parties and

---

[114] Los Angeles Times. Patrick Goldstein, Friday, June 17, 2011.

organizations. I theorize about the causes of this bias, and argue empirically that, while demographic variables are not completely irrelevant, Hollywood liberalism is primarily a function of high, publicly visible incomes, and family connections. Neither religion nor birthplace effects seem to affect political activity in the film business."" [115]

---

[115] Kendall, Todd D. Walker, John E. *An Empirical Analysis of Political Activity in Hollywood*. Department of Economics, Clemson University, October, 2007.

The authors identified Hollywood political donors and their recipients:

Table 2: Largest Contributors in Sample

Actors	Total Contributions	Non-Actors	Total Contributions
Michael Douglas	396,000	Steven Spielberg	285,400
Paul Newman	76,450	Rob Reiner	274,970
Alec Baldwin	73,000	Richard Donner	35,600
Danny DeVito	64,500	Garry Marshall	29,100
Robin Williams	61,000	Gary Ross	26,000
Ellen Barkin	60,000	Barry Levinson	21,000
Bette Midler	57,500	Frank Darabont	19,750
Chevy Chase	57,500	Brian Robbins	17,000
Edward Norton	53,000	Nora Ephron	16,850
Robert DeNiro	35,000	Cameron Crowe	14,700
Candice Bergen	34,500	Peter Farrelly	13,400
Tom Cruise	30,500	Oliver Stone	13,250
Tom Hanks	30,000	Edward Zwick	11,400
Kevin Spacey	29,000	Steven Soderbergh	10,000
Brendan Fraser	27,000	Taylor Hackford	9,900
Richard Dreyfuss	25,400	Harold Ramis	8,750
Ethan Hawke	25,000	Doug Liman	8,500
Renee Zellweger	24,000	Michael Mann	8,150
Nicole Kidman	19,500	Robert Zemeckis	8,150
Christopher Guest	18,500	William Friedkin	8,000
Donal Logue	18,000	Brett Ratner	7,950
Paul Reiser	16,500	Martin Scorsese	7,900
Jeff Bridges	15,500	Ron Howard	7,000
Dustin Hoffman	15,000	David Mamet	7,000
Kevin Bacon	14,500	Betty Thomas	5,600

Table 3: Political Organizations or Politicians
Receiving Largest Amount of Contributions

Political Organization Or Politician	Office	Total Contributions
Democratic National Committee	N/A	742,100
Democratic Senatorial Campaign Committee	Senate	475,650
Democratic Congressional Campaign Committee	House	274,650
Kerry, John (D)	Senate, Pres.	174,250
Directors' Guild PAC	N/A	93,750
Clinton, Hillary (D)	Senate	71,420
Boxer, Barbara (D)	Senate	66,500
Gore, Al (D)	President	52,280
Clooney, Nick (D)	House	45,500
Dean, Howard (D)	President	41,000
Gephardt, Richard (D)	House, Pres.	34,000
Daschle, Thomas (D)	Senate, Pres.	33,250
New York State Democratic Committee	N/A	30,000
Clark, Wesley (D)	President	27,500
Schumer, Charles (D)	Senate	26,000
Bradley, Bill (D)	President	24,625
Rangel, Charles (D)	House	18,250
Obama, Barack (D)	Senate	17,500
Dodd, Christopher (D)	Senate	15,500
Gordon, Barry (D)	House	14,000

One of the more fascinating aspects of the progressive virus's ability to distort reality is its ability to compartmentalize and rationalize glaring inconsistencies in behavior, including blatant hypocrisy.

Author Jason Mattera cited numerous examples of what he terms hypocrisy among the Hollywood elite. A couple of notable examples, according to Mattera, include Barbra Streisand. Streisand called attention to a "Global Warming Emergency" in 2005 but pays $22,000 a year to water her lawn. Harrison Ford, the vice chairman of Conservation International, owns seven airplanes. Mattera quoted Ford as saying: "I often fly up the coast for a cheeseburger." [116] The carbon footprint of the Hollywood elite, paired with their almost universal hysteria concerning global warming, requires an Oscar winning ability to rationalize hypocritical behavior.

As we know, forced equilibrium is a hallmark edict of the progressive virus. Discriminating between groups or individuals is tantamount to, according to the elite, fascism. Hollywood's elite, like their progressive brethren everywhere, demand equivalency in everything, but only when it is convenient for them. Nowhere do we see convenient equilibrium more clearly demonstrated than in Hollywood. Hollywood's progressive

---

[116] Mattera, Jason. Hollywood Hypocrites. The Devastating Truth about Obama's Biggest Backers. Threshold Editions, March 13, 2012.

colony is a supporter and promoter of affirmative action, quotas, racial, gender and any other equality they can *impose on others*, but not themselves.

One area where Hollywood is conveniently out of equilibrium has to do with gender.

> "[T]here are more females serving on the United States Supreme Court than there are writing for The Late Show with David Letterman, The Jay Leno Show, and The Tonight Show with Conan O'Brien combined. Out of the 50 or so comedy writers working on these programs, exactly zero are women. It would be funny if it weren't true." [117]

Writers for television, likewise, somehow escape Hollywood's elite's demand for social justice so readily imposed on others.

> "In the 2006-2007 television season, 35 percent of the writers of broadcast network, prime-time programs were women, according to an annual study by San Diego State University's Center for the Study of Women in Television and Film. In the 2010-2011 season, that number had dropped by

---

[117] Vanity Fair. Sex Matters, Reporter Neil Scovell. October 27, 2009.

more than half, to 15 percent. What happened?"
118

Writers on the John Stewart Daily Show have been, over the years, almost totally made up of men. Where are the women? We agree with the only honest retort is that hiring the most talented writers, regardless of gender, is the way to insure a successful show.

In late 2011 "Occupy Wall Street" took to the streets. Their mantra pitted the 1% against the 99%. The protesters were purportedly made up of the 99%. The 1% was portrayed, for the most part, as greedy capitalists who exploited the "people" and who were known to buy power in Washington.

You would be hard-pressed to name one of the Hollywood elite who was not sympathetic to the "occupiers." Talk shows airing during the period of the occupation almost always asked their Hollywood A-listers to give their opinion on the Occupy Wall Street protesters. I can't think of one of the Hollywood elite who made any disparaging remarks about the occupiers. And what is equally fascinating is that I cannot think of one "occupier" who voiced a negative opinion of the 1-percenters who make up the Hollywood elite. The Hollywood elite reside in gated mansions, have chauffeurs, private chefs and, for the

---

118 Huffington Post. Reporter: Maureen Ryan. September 8th 2011.

most part, would not be caught dead wearing anything but haute couture, yes *those* 1-percenters somehow escaped the wrath of the occupiers.

And speaking of 1-percenters, John Stewart, host of the *Daily Show* on Comedy Central, has made a career out of skewering the rich. In January of 2012 he took on Republican presidential candidate Mitt Romney. Stewart railed against the fact that Romney accrues almost $57,000 dollar per day! What Stewart's fawning audience was oblivious to is that according to the website Celebrity Net Worth, Stewart and his wife make approximately 15 million dollars per year and have an estimated net worth at $80 million dollars, that's $41,000 per day!

Stewart, who is 49 years of age, is on schedule to outpace the foil of his satire and ridicule, Mitt Romney, who is age 65 as of 2012. By the time Stewart is 65, if he continues to make the same amount of money, his net worth will be $320 million dollars. Stewart and his wife have trusts named after their dogs and cats. These trusts own multiple mansions and opulent properties.

We do not begrudge Mr. Stewart his financial success. As a matter of fact, we congratulate him. Our point here is that Stewart's hypocrisy is stunning when one realizes that the shtick that is Stewart's stock in trade relies upon pillorying the rich, pretending to identify with the 99% and performing this slight of hand before a fawning and obviously gullible audience while exhibiting not one iota of self-reflection.

Hollywood's elite is made up of some very talented people. Not only are they talented with it comes to presentation skills and charisma, those in front of the camera are better looking, for the most part, than the 99%. Many actor's and actress's raison d'être is that he or she is charismatic and physically attractive. Casting directors discriminate between the talented and have-not talent with cruel and insensitive efficiency. Producers and directors discriminate against the ugly every day. Where is the egalitarianism? Ugly looking people make it before the camera only when directors need an ugly person to play the role of the murderer, miscreant or pervert. Casting directors are ruthlessly efficient in culling the haves from the have-nots when it comes to their business, but not yours.

The Hollywood elite are very discriminating when it comes to who they date—no forced equilibrium here, no siree. When is the last time you saw a male matinee idol with an unattractive, average looking mate? How many of Hollywood's elite male stars date or marry much younger women? Hollywood's so called progressive "Cougars" engage in the same obsession with younger men. Interesting, isn't it, that Hollywood's most vocal male posh-progressives seem to be commitment challenged and only date much younger, beautiful women? These are the same people spouting progressive dogma and who get into fist-fights over who gets top billing or when photographers dare encroach their personal space. These are the same progressive stars who habitually preen themselves in front of the mirror like nervous cockatoos or throw hissy fits if they are denied some privilege by an "average" person.

In the mid-nineties I had the opportunity to talk with one of the producers of the television show "Three's Company." Teddy Bergman was one of the people involved in the constructive dismissal of Suzanne Somers. According to Mr. Bergman, Somers, accompanied by her husband/manager, walked into his office and demanded more money. According to Bergman, Somers expressed that she was the star of the show, and therefore warranted a bigger paycheck and more creative control.

That act on the part of Somers represented a challenge to authority, not only a challenge to the show's producers, but to all of the Hollywood elite who run the place. "The talent can't control the show," said Mr. Bergman. Somers has noted that she felt like the producers were intent upon "hanging a nun the courtyard" to teach her and any other actor a lesson who would dare challenge Hollywood's iron fist authority. No "spread the wealth" here.

Then there is Al Gore. The former vice president went Hollywood when he publicized his slide show on global warming, now termed climate change. Gore is estimated to have made millions and millions of dollars advocating on behalf of a planet that, according to Gore, "has a fever." Was it the planet or something else that had a fever?

According to Quality Metrics, a purveyor of information about meteorology:

> "Since campaigning for stricter carbon emission rules and trading, Mr. Gore has also invested millions of dollars in green energy and environmental business ventures, like solar energy, carbon trading markets, and waterless technologies. Also, his political sidekicks have the inside scoop and are following his lead. House Speaker Nancy Pelosi and Robert F. Kennedy Jr. are not only leading the senate towards energy-saving policies, they also are investing their personal funds in Gores' energy venture. [W]hen Mr. Gore left government in early 2001, he had assets of less than $2 million. Since that time, his environmental lobbying and his private investments have made him one of the richest Americans of the decade. He will make billions of

dollars off global warming and the green energy movement." [119]

In 2010 Gore made a real estate purchase that even made the 1-percenters envious.

"Al and Tipper Gore have picked up a $8.875M luxury getaway in Montecito, CA; a swanky zip code that has attracted big name residents like Oprah Winfrey, Steve Martin, and Kirk Douglas. Records show that the approximately 6,500 sq. foot home boasts 6 bedrooms, 9 bathrooms, a large pool house, 6 fireplaces, wood framed French doors, and carved stone detailing throughout." [120]

Vice President Gore's 10,000-square-foot mansion in Belle Meade, Tennessee was retrofitted with solar panels a few years ago, after he had been criticized for the amount of energy the home used. And speaking of the energy:

"In his documentary, the former Vice President calls on Americans to conserve energy by reducing electricity consumption at home. The average household in America consumes 10,656 kilowatt-hours (kWh) per year, according to the

---

[119] Quality Metrics: Understanding Meteorology, 2011.
[120] Huffington Post. Los Angeles Real Estate, May 17, 2006.

Department of Energy. In 2006, Gore devoured nearly 221,000 kWh–more than 20 times the national average. Last August alone, Gore burned through 22,619 kWh–guzzling more than twice the electricity in one month than an average American family uses in an entire year. As a result of his energy consumption, Gore's average monthly electric bill topped $1,359. Since the release of An Inconvenient Truth, Gore's energy consumption has increased from an average of 16,200 kWh per month in 2005, to 18,400 kWh per month in 2006. Gore's extravagant energy use does not stop at his electric bill. Natural gas bills for Gore's mansion and guest house averaged $1,080 per month last year. 'As the spokesman of choice for the global warming movement, Al Gore has to be willing to walk the walk, not just talk the talk, when it comes to home energy use,' said Tennessee Center for Policy Research President Drew Johnson. In total, Gore paid nearly $30,000 in combined electricity and natural gas bills for his Nashville estate in 2006." [121]

---

[121] Tennessee Center for Policy Research, by Drew Johnson, February 26, 2007.

Vice President Gore also travels by private jet to his showings of An Inconvenient Truth. How convenient for him. In case there is some doubt that Vice President Gore has "gone Hollywood," he divorced his wife of 40 years, Tipper, in June of 2010. Gore now joins a long list of Hollywood's commitment challenged elite male stars. It didn't take long for Mr. Gore to fall prey to Hollywood's anti-marriage and anti-commitment progressive culture.

In August of 2008 the Parents Television Council published a 17-page report that studied Hollywood's impact on marriage. Here is what the researchers concluded:

> "The PTC study concluded that many in Hollywood are actively seeking to undermine marriage by consistently showing it in a negative manner." Furthermore, the study expressed grave concern about the rapid increase in network television's preoccupation with once-taboo sexual subjects. For example, references to bestiality, incest, necrophilia, pedophilia, transsexuals/transvestites, and threesomes outnumbered references to sex within marriage 27 to 1 on NBC. The same network had as many depictions of adults having sex with minors as there were depictions of sex between married

partners. The good news about ABC was that they had the most references to marital sex. The bad news is that a significant number of the references were negative. By contrast, almost none of ABC's references to non-marital sex were negative." [122]

Welcome to Hollywood Mr. Vice President, you'll be welcomed with open arms and fit right in.

---

[122] The Ethics and Religious Liberty Counsel. Parents Television Counsel Study. August 14, 2008.

CHAPTER FOURTEEN

Political Correctness

POLITICALLY CORRECT SPEECH IS nothing more than the progressive virus shielding itself from destruction. PC is also used as a progressive weapon. PC is the progressive virus's way of neutralizing a person who dares to speak the truth by attaching a socially unacceptable label on the person posing a threat; for example, racist, homophobe, Islamophobe, polluter, misogynist, fascist, etc. The progressive virus attaches labels to threats, with one purpose in mind, to stifle speech and protect itself from that which is lethal to it, i.e., the truth. The virus could not care less that the label they attach is undeserved. Ever hear of the label Christanophobe? Didn't think so.

Truth, when spoken to a progressive, poses a lethal threat to the virus. I saw this vividly demonstrated when I was still a student. One fall day professor Coulson told his students this: "Pink lungs are good and diseased brown lungs are bad, no matter what you may say." A progressive infected student yelled out: "fascist!"

Why would speaking the truth pose such a threat? Because professor Coulson boldly asserted that there is objective good and bad, and that some things are "good" and some things are "bad" regardless of man's perverted perceptions.

Bill Lind, writing for Accuracy in Academia, traced the origins of the PC movement:

> "If we look at it analytically, if we look at it historically, we quickly find out exactly what it is. Political Correctness is cultural Marxism. It is Marxism translated from economic into cultural terms. It is an effort that goes back not to the 1960s and the hippies and the peace movement, but back to World War I. If we compare the basic tenets of Political Correctness with classical Marxism the parallels are very obvious.
>
> First of all, both are totalitarian ideologies. The totalitarian nature of Political Correctness is revealed nowhere more clearly than on college campuses, many of which at this point are small ivy covered North Koreas, where the student or faculty member who dares to cross any of the lines set up by the gender feminist or the homosexual-rights activists, or the local black or Hispanic group, or any of the other sainted

"victims" groups that PC revolves around, quickly find themselves in judicial trouble. Within the small legal system of the college, they face formal charges – some star-chamber proceeding – and punishment. That is a little look into the future that Political Correctness intends for the nation as a whole." [123]

Underlying Marxism is the progressive virus. As we have demonstrated, those infected with the progressive virus are attracted to Marxism, Communism and Socialism. When successful at getting what they want, American progressives morph into European socialists, then Marxists, then communists, in the same way a tadpole morphs into a frog. The tadpole is a nascent version of what it already has within it—a frog. Progressives are totalitarian by their very nature. Progressives regulate, control, oversee and commandeer everything. And the one thing they recognize as critical to their success, they must control speech. This is because within some speech lies a virulent threat to the progressive virus, the truth. In 1991 Richard Ebeling, writing for Freedom Daily, had this to say:

"[M]any of the proponents of "politically correct thinking" in American academia are refugees and

---

[123] Lind, Bill. Accuracy in Academia. *The Origins of Political Correctness*. February 5, 2000.

exiles from the leftist political causes of the 1960s — for example, they who resisted American intervention in Vietnam because they supported socialist revolution in the Third World. They protested against "the establishment' at home because they hated capitalism and saw themselves as the vanguard of a coming "people's democracy" that would replace the existing "fascist America"; and they protested because they hated the "commercial society" and resented the "oppression" of market relationships." [124]

The PC movement has taken hold in America. So much so that even innocent uses of some words are strictly forbade. Jay Karlson, writing for ListVerse, compiled the following examples of Political Correctness

- *Xbox Live recently banned Josh Moore for violating its gamers' code of conduct. His offense? Filling out his Xbox Live profile. You see, Mr. Moore lives in West Virginia. More specifically, in FORT GAY, West Virginia. As Microsoft says, the word "gay" is always offensive. Never*

---

[124] Eberling, Richard. Freedom Daily. *Politically Correct Thinking and State Education*. April, 1991.

mind that several US townships incorporate the word into their name, many people have "Gay" as a first or last name, and some homosexuals do identify themselves as "gay." No, Microsoft obviously had a wise guy in their midst, and he had to go. So, despite a total lack of customer complaints, Microsoft froze Moore's account and warned him that he could lose his prepaid subscription if he badgered Customer Service further. Fort Gay Mayor, David Thompson, tried to intervene, but was told that the city's name didn't matter; the word "gay" was inappropriate in any context.

- In 2007, Santa Clauses in Sydney, Australia, were forced to revolt for the right to say "Ho Ho Ho", the traditional laugh of jolly old St. Nick. It turns out that their employer, the recruitment firm Westaff (that supplies hundreds of Santas across Australia), told all trainees that "ho ho ho" could frighten children and be derogatory to women. Why? Because it was too close to the American (not Australian, mind you) slang for prostitute. Instead, the Santas were instructed to lower their voices and say "Ha ha ha". Westaff relented only after the story broke nationally, deciding to leave the belly laughs "up to the discretion of Santa himself.

- *In 2003, Dennis Tafoya, director of the LA County affirmative action office, issued a memo describing an "exhaustive search" for any computer equipment labeled "master" and "slave". He also stated that all offending labels should be replaced with more appropriate terminology. Purchasing officials subsequently requested that all suppliers cease using labels deemed "unacceptable and offensive"—the first step of a creeping labeling ban. The county began their investigation after ONE worker saw a videotape machine bearing the labels and filed a discrimination complaint with the Office of Affirmative Action Compliance. However, "master" and "slave" are common terms for primary and secondary hard drives in the computer industry, and have been used without complaint for decades. Due to overwhelming negative publicity and a near revolt from suppliers, LA County's Division Manager of Purchasing and Contract Services promised there would be no ban on computer equipment based on current labeling practices.*

- *Uncle Remus is the American Aesop, and we're losing this literary treasure in our libraries and cinemas. For example, Disney's delightful "Song of the South" hasn't been in official circulation since 2001, and likely won't be*

ANTHONY NAPOLEON

anytime soon. The general objection to the film (which features the Uncle Remus stories) lies in the portrayal of African-Americans in the live action sequences. Many mistakenly believe that the movie sugarcoats slavery, but, if any of the self-appointed PC censors had actually READ the book, they'd know that the Uncle Remus stories are set AFTER the Civil War and AFTER the abolition of slavery. This is evident in the film, when Uncle Remus freely leaves the plantation with no fear of reprisal at all. Walt Disney assumed people already knew this, and thought explaining it would be over the heads of most children (it is a kid's movie, after all). But, depending on the PC crowd to read is a losing bet, and "Song of the South" remains locked in a vault.

- *Administrators at a California high school sent five students home after they refused to remove their American flag T-shirts on Cinco de Mayo, the Mexican Day of Independence. That's right, kids, you can't wear your country's flag in your country, lest it offend someone celebrating the holiday of a different country. The story began when Assistant Principal, Miguel Rodriguez, asked two of the five teens to remove their American flag bandanas. The boys complied, but were still taken to the principal's office for a chat. One of the boys told NBC*

228

"They said we could wear it on any other day, but today is sensitive to Mexican-Americans because it's supposed to be their holiday, so we were not allowed to wear it." They are right. It might be a little insensitive to wear an American flag shirt on Cinco De Mayo– if we were in MEXICO.

- *And it is an important holiday—IN MEXICO. School District Superintendent Wesley Smith later described the incident as "extremely unfortunate" and said the matter is still under investigation.*

- *The Maine Human Rights Commission has proposed banning ANY gender divisions in public schools after ruling that, under the Maine Human Rights Act, a school discriminated against a 12-year-old transgender boy by denying him access to the girls' bathroom. Think about that last part: after denying HIM access to the GIRL'S bathroom. As a result, in the near future, Maine schools may have no gender differences in sports teams, school clubs, bathrooms, or locker rooms. So, how many horny Maine boys do you think are working on a "transgender" scam to get into the girl's locker room? Hint: it rhymes with "all", because it is "all". The commission promises to issue guidelines on how to deal with the thorny particulars. I'm sure it will make fascinating reading.*

- *In 2008, a Carmel, Indiana, school bus driver, Betty Campbell, overheard little Rachel Zimmer saying that she couldn't vote for presidential candidate Barak Obama because of his positions on abortion and gay marriage. That led to unsubstantiated allegations that she said that other students would go to Hell, which Zimmer strongly denies. When Campbell heard the allegations (again, unsubstantiated) she stopped the bus and delivered a politically correct sermon on tolerance to her captive audience, who probably just wanted to go home and play Xbox before their moms and dads came home. The security camera caught it all on tape, including Campbell's conversations with another student. She probed this student for racist allegations, threatening to "eat Zimmer alive" and calling her "a stupid little bigot". It gets worse. After dropping Zimmer at home, Campbell completed her route and then RETURNED to the Zimmer home, ordering Zimmer and her sister back into the EMPTY school bus (without parental knowledge or consent) for more browbeating. She again lectured Zimmer about her opinions on gay marriage and reduced the girl to tears. After seeing the tape, Zimmer's parents went ballistic, saying: "That's not someone looking out for someone. That's someone out to get somebody."*

Carmel Clay Schools refused to fire or even discipline Campbell, stating that she was working within "the scope of her employment." The family has since filed a civil lawsuit.

- *In 2006, the Duke Lacrosse team held a party and hired two strippers for the event. Not impressed with the talent on display, they rudely sent dancer Crystal Gail Mangum and her friend packing after a few songs. Payment was an issue, but witnesses say they departed safely. However, Mangum later accused three players of raping her at the party. What followed was a PC free-for-all involving the university, the press, and the district attorney's office. Presumption of guilt was total. The university cancelled the remaining lacrosse season. 88 faculty members published a rushed full-page ad in the newspaper siding with the alleged 'victim,' and decrying institutional racism at Duke. Three players were indicted for first degree forcible rape and kidnapping, while several others were pilloried in the school newspapers and complained that professors were unfairly failing them. Other players transferred to lesser schools, glad to get a degree at all. District attorney Mike Nifong wanted in on the rich college boy takedown, so he ignored the DNA tests that failed to connect anyone on the team with*

Mangum, and used a 'suspects only' photo list for her to ID her assailants. Eventually, scores of inconsistencies in Magnum's testimony came flooding through, including prior false accusations of rape, no corroboration from her friend at the party, and an ever-changing events timeline. One newspaper determined Mangum was telling at least five different stories at any given time. Worst of all, one player was videotaped by an ATM camera miles away at the exact time he was supposed to be raping Mangum. The tide had turned– North Carolina law and Duke were looking decidedly foolish. So on April 11, 2007, the Attorney General dropped all charges and declared the three players innocent–victims of a "tragic rush to accuse."

- *District Attorney Mike Nifong was later disbarred. The ex-players are seeking unspecified damages from the City of Durham, and Duke has already completed several legal settlements. The NCAA even reinstated the players' athletic eligibility, although most had already graduated. The group of 88 professors has yet to publish an apology or retraction of their original ad. Miss Mangum was later arrested in 2010, in a separate case, and has been indicted for attempted first-degree murder, five counts of arson, assault and battery, communicating threats, three counts of misdemeanor child abuse, injury to personal property, identity theft and resisting a public officer.*

- *Political Correctness can have deadly consequences, even for an army at war. In November 2009, US Army Psychologist Nidal Malik Hasan killed 13 people (one pregnant) by opening fire on a US Army base, all while shouting "God is Great" in Arabic (a misappropriation of Muslim prayers, but used in the 9/11 attacks). How could anything like this happen on a military base? Unbelievably, the Pentagon knew of Hasan's emails to radical imams, and his increasingly bizarre policy recommendations for Muslims serving in the US armed forces. Many coworkers and colleagues referred to him as a "ticking time bomb." Red flags appeared everywhere showing that Hasan was seriously conflicted about being a Muslim in the US military, but the Army's middle management ignored these signals because they were "afraid to be accused of profiling somebody." That PC fear may have cost 13 people their lives.* [125]

Mr. Karlson's last entry provides us a teaching moment. Besides the existential dangers associated with the PC movement, millions upon millions of human beings have been killed because

---

[125] ListVerse. By Jay Karlson. 10 Ridiculous Case of Political Correctness. October 26, 2010.

the progressives found no other way to stifle truth-telling speech.

In the former USSR, progressives controlled speech, ideas, images and re-wrote history.

"All media in the Soviet Union were controlled by the state including television and radio broadcasting, newspaper, magazine and book publishing. This was achieved by state ownership of all production facilities, thus making all those employed in media state employees. This extended to the fine arts including the theater, opera and ballet. Art and music was controlled by ownership of distribution and performance venues. Censorship was backed in cases where performances did not meet with the favor of the Soviet leadership with newspaper campaigns against offending material and sanctions applied though party controlled professional organizations. In the case of book publishing a manuscript had to pass censorship and the decision of a state owned publishing house to publish and distribute the book. Books which met with official favor, for example, the collected speeches of Leonid Brezhnev were printed in vast quantities while less favored literary material might be published in limited numbers and not distributed widely. Popular escapist literature such as the popular best-sellers, mysteries and romances which form the bulk of Western publishing was nearly non-existent. Possession and use of copying machines was tightly controlled in order to hinder production and distribution of samizdat, illegal self-published books and magazines. Possession of even a single samizdat manuscript such as a book by Andrei Sinyavsky was a serious crime which might involve a visit from the KGB. Another outlet for works which did not find favor with the authorities was publishing abroad. It was the practice of libraries in the Soviet Union to restrict access to back issues of journals and newspapers more than three years old. "[126]

In modern-day Cuba we find a draconian "gagging law."

"Promulgated in February 1999, the "88 Law" – soon nicknamed the "gagging law" in dissident circles – weighs like the Sword of Damocles over any person who "collaborates, by any means whatsoever, with radio or television programs, magazines or any

---

[126] Wikipedia. Censorship in the Soviet Union.

other foreign media or provides information considered likely to serve US policy. The law provides for very heavy sentences: up to 20 years' imprisonment, confiscation of all personal belongings and fines up to 100,000 pesos (close to 4,800 dollars, while the average Cuban salary is 250 pesos or 12 dollars per month). The law provides for punishment for the promotion, organization or encouragement of, or the participation in meetings or demonstrations. "[127] This law is the latest in a long history of the oppression of free speech in Cuba.

In April of 2003, 29 journalists were imprisoned in Castro's Cuba.

> "On April 7, courts across the island announced prison sentences for the 29 journalists, ranging from 14 to 27 years. González Alfonso and prominent journalist and poet Raúl Rivero were each sentenced to 20 years in prison. According to the prosecutor's petition, the two journalists were accused of, among other charges, creating the journalists' organization Sociedad de Periodistas Manuel Márquez Sterling and its "subversive" magazine, De Cuba. Rivero and González Alfonso were tried under Article 91 of the Penal Code, which imposes lengthy prison

---

[127] Bienvenue a Cuba. Freedom of Speech in Cuba.

sentences or death for those who act against "the independence or the territorial integrity of the State." Other journalists were also prosecuted for violating Law 88 for the Protection of Cuba's National Independence and Economy, which imposes up to 20 years in prison for anyone who commits "acts that in agreement with imperialist interests are aimed at subverting the internal order of the Nation and destroy its political, economic, and social system. The journalists remained imprisoned in several jails administered by the State Security Department until April 24, 2003, when most were sent to jails located hundreds of miles from their homes." [128]

During the rule of the Khmer Rouge in Cambodia, mass murder was the order of the day.

"The Cambodian genocide of 1975-1979, in which approximately 1.7 million people lost their lives (21% of the country's population), was one of the worst human tragedies of the last century. As in the Ottoman Empire during the Armenian genocide, in Nazi Germany, and more recently in

---

[128] Committee to Protect Journalists. Crackdown on the Independent Press in Cuba. February 14, 2003.

East Timor, Guatemala, Yugoslavia, and Rwanda, the Khmer Rouge regime headed by Pol Pot combined extremist ideology with ethnic animosity and a diabolical disregard for human life to produce repression, misery, and murder on a massive scale. "[129]

The compulsive quest for equal outcomes, that is, forced equilibrium, drove the Khmer Rouge to commit genocide.

Modern day North Korea is, like its progressive infected brethren everywhere, deeply vested in controlling speech.

"North Koreans live in the most censored country in the world, a new analysis by the Committee to Protect Journalists has found. The world's deepest information void, communist North Korea has no independent journalists, and all radio and television receivers sold in the country are locked to government-specified frequencies. Burma, Turkmenistan, Equatorial Guinea, and Libya round out the top five nations on CPJ's list of the "10 Most Censored Countries." [130]

In the United States, those infected with the progressive virus face an immune system barrier originally designed by America's

---

[129] Yale University. Cambodian Genocide Project. 2010.
[130] Committee to Protect Journalists. 10 Most Censored Countries. May, 2006.

founders to guarantee "free speech." Americans are quick to give lip service to the notion of free speech, but often do not stop to think about what was going on in the minds of the founding fathers when they wrote the First Amendment to the Constitution in 1789. The British Monarchy, like all totalitarian regimes, squelched the speaking of truth.

Enter John Peter Zenger. John Peter Zenger was a German immigrant and publisher of *The New York Daily Journal*. Zenger's newspaper was considered, at the time, (1730s) to be pro-colonist and anti-Royal. It was financially supported by the Morrisites, a political party that stood in opposition to many of the Tory-like policies of its political rival, the Court party. Some of Zenger's more threatening editorials included exposés on a British Governor by the name of William Cosby. In particular, Cosby's rigging of the 1734 elections; Cosby's personal use of tax monies and Cosby's illegal appropriation of Indian lands, among others.

In November 1734, Governor Cosby ordered his men to burn four editions of the New York Daily Journal. These editions contained the allegedly seditious, truth-telling material that so bothered Governor Cosby. On November 17, 1734, Zenger was arrested for "seditious libel" against Cosby. This arrest took place despite the fact that a New York grand jury, consisting of American colonists, refused to indict Zenger. During Zenger's incarceration awaiting trial, his wife Anna, in a display of bravery and patriotism, continued printing the newspaper.

The Zenger trial provides us with a classic example of how far vested interests can and will go to attack the speaking of truth in the absence of a Constitutional guarantee to speak the truth. Governor Cosby disbarred the local defense counsel for Zenger. In response, the Morrisites hired Andrew Hamilton, a talented trial lawyer from Philadelphia, to defend Zenger. Even Cosby concluded that he could not attack Hamilton's credibility, and feeling that he could sway the jury with his own lawyer, a sinecure of the King himself, Cosby permitted the trial to go forward. Zenger's lawyer argued that the newspaper couldn't be punished unless what it had printed was falsely seditious. Hamilton created in that trial a concept we all have come to accept as a given: The truth can never be libelous. [131]

It was the Zenger trial and similar assaults upon truth telling by the British Monarchy and their agents in the colonies that motivated James Madison to draft the First Amendment to the Constitution.

"Madison's version of the speech and press clauses, introduced in the House of Representatives on June 8, 1789, provided: "The

[131] Michael Kammen, *Colonial New York: A History*. New York: Oxford University Press, 1975.

people shall not be deprived or abridged of their right to speak, to write, or to publish their sentiments; and the freedom of the press, as one of the great bulwarks of liberty, shall be inviolable." [132]

The First Amendment to the Constitution has not stopped progressives from acting like their Royal brethren. Progressives believe that they create reality. America's founding father's reality may not, in fact certainly is not, their reality.

When PC pressure doesn't fully protect the progressive virus from truth telling, calls to limit the First Amendment result. Senator Charles Schumer, a progressive from New York, made the following pitch to rewrite James Madison's 1789 First Amendment:

"I believe there ought to be limits because the First Amendment is not absolute. No amendment is absolute. You can't scream 'fire' falsely in a crowded theater. We have libel laws. We have anti-pornography laws. All of those are limits on the First Amendment. Well, what could be more important than the wellspring of our democracy?

---

[132] FindLaw. Cases & Codes: U.S. Constitution: Amendments: First Amendment,
Annotations p. 6.

And certain limits on First Amendment rights that if left unfettered, destroy the equality — any semblance of equality in our democracy — of course would be allowed by the Constitution. And the new theorists on the Supreme Court who don't believe that, I am not sure where their motivation comes from, but they are just so wrong. They are just so wrong." [133]

Progressives have had remarkable success quelling free speech using their Trojan-Horse method of packaging totalitarian control within an attractive package. Who, after all, is in favor of "hate" speech? Who favors racism, misogyny, sexism, dirty air or unsafe water? Who would listen to a racist, misogynist, fascist or polluter, after all?

Progressives use a method of speech control that mirrors the methods employed by Muslims in their quest to instill Islamic law. "Creeping Sha'ria" has been copied by progressives, and now takes the form of "creeping totalitarianism."

Progressives have been brilliant at "creeping" community organizing, infiltrating public schools, framing political discourse and yes, controlling speech and ideas that would undermine their agenda. Creeping socialism has been termed Fabian socialism.

---

[133] Senator Charles Schumer, Democrat, New York. Speech on the Senate Floor, July 16, 2012.

Fabian progressives trust the effectiveness of an incremental, step-by-step destruction of traditional America that may obviate the need to create a violent revolution.

Progressives not only control speech, they use PC to attach a Scarlet Letter to anyone who poses a threat to them. Progressives are quick to pull the trigger on attaching the Scarlet Letter to their enemies.

Progressive frequently affix the suffix "phobe" to any one of their pet social causes, groups or class of individuals. Any person who threatens one of their many pet social causes, groups or class of individuals has that suffix-added label attached to them. That suffix (originally Phobos) means fear or frightened of. The "phobe" label is designed to diminish and shut up anyone to whom it is attached because it suggests that the person to whom they attach the label is afraid (unnecessarily of course) of the issue, group or class of people they are criticizing and not that the criticism or comments are meritorious. *The label is designed to forestall a discussion of the merits of the challenger's comments or observations.*

How "hair trigger" is the PC police? They are unbelievably quick on the draw. For example, while it is perfectly acceptable to say: John Fitzgerald Kennedy, Lyndon Baines Johnson or William Jefferson Clinton, if anyone dares to say Barack Hussein

Obama the Scarlett Letter of Racist or Islamophobe is plastered on the forehead of the speaker.

Those to whom the label "homophobe" is typically attached are not afraid of homosexuals; most of them simply disagree with the promotion of the homosexual lifestyle for the culture at large. Catholics, who repeatedly stress that their collective problem with homosexuality is with the behavior and not the person, are still labeled with the "phobe" suffix. To be sure, there are people who are afraid of gay people simply because they are gay. However, because of the overuse of the Scarlett Letter by progressives, true homophobes are lost in a sea of people wearing unwarranted "homophobe" labels. PC labeling makes it virtually impossible to make any observation about or constructive criticism of any progressive favored group, individual or class of people.

The Scarlet Letter "Islamophobe" is another classic example of the manipulative use of labels to squelch speech. Those who discuss, for example, Islamic demographics or Sha'ria law, the threats posed by mosques in New York City (please see the bi-partisan 9/11 Commission's report), are anything but fearful. If any group does not deserve the "phobe" label, it is this group. On the other hand, those progressives who pander to Muslims at every turn while making derisive, snarky criticisms of Christians, whenever afforded the opportunity, deserve the label of fearful. Was Salmon Rushdie an Islamophobe? Were the writers on South-Park Islamophobes? Is the Pope a homophobe? Are progressives Christianophobes?

The offender of PC is often forced to genuflect in the form of an "apology." **Genuflection is not another word for "apology."** Genuflection is an act of submission to progressives and should never be made under PC pressure. If an apology is genuine, then it should come from the heart and not take the form of a genuflection to the PC police.

Progressives betray their true agenda when they "selectively" control speech and the affixation of labels. It is clear that the PC police provide immunity to other progressives, no matter what they say. Progressives tolerate other progressive's acts of racism, misogyny, fascism, anti-gay tirades, environmental exploitation and almost any other non-PC behavior.

Virtually without exception, if a progressive attacks someone who poses a threat to progressive dogma, then that person can be safely attacked without hearing a peep from the thought police. For instance, Sara Palin's views are "anathema to progressive ambitions." This means that she is fair game, i.e., you can say almost any vile thing about her or her family and you will get a pass. Bill Maher has called Sara Palin a "slut." He has also used the term "cunt" to describe the former Governor. He also said this about the former Governor of Alaska's family:

"...While we were off, Sarah Palin agreed to do commentary at Fox News. Which is actually very similar to her day job – talking to a baby with Down (sic) Syndrome."

Maher has also called Palin a "dumb twat." But when it came to Maher's contribution of $1 million dollars to a progressive political action committee, dedicated to the re-election of President Obama, you could have heard a pin drop from his progressive brethren. Maher regularly has as his guests sitting members of Congress, media elite and members of academia. Belittling him as merely a comedian is nonsense. For one thing, comedians are often important social commentators. For another, Maher is an important contributor to social and political discourse

Maher is not alone. Progressive infected David Letterman took aim at Mrs. Palin and her daughter. Letterman focused upon the Palin's attendance at a Yankee's game while visiting New York City. Palin was honored by a special needs group at the game. Letterman referred to Palin as having the style of a "slutty flight attendant." Letterman also took a shot Palin's daughter.

"One awkward moment for Sarah Palin at the Yankee game, during the seventh inning, her daughter was knocked up by Alex Rodriguez."

Palin attended that game with her 14 year-old daughter.

On the other hand, when Rush Limbaugh called Sandra Fluke a prostitute because she demanded that her sexual behavior be paid for in the form of birth control pills, and despite the fact that Limbaugh thought better of his comments and apologized within 24 hours of saying those words, he was castigated 24/7 by progressives in the mass media who, like a playful dog with a bone, would not let go of the story. Boycotts, calls for his firing and demands that stations drop the Limbaugh show from their lineup became the focus of progressives everywhere. The story only stopped after progressives had squeezed every last drop out of the incident.

Just to be clear, Bill Maher has retained somewhat of a viable immune system that has protected him from completely succumbing to the progressive virus. He has retained some ability to discriminate. For example, he demonstrated his ability to discriminate on the subject of disproportionate threats posed by various religions. When he displayed his ability to discriminate on his show *Real Time*, his progressive guests frowned and scowled at him.

Also, by citing the behavior of Letterman, Maher and others, I am not acceding to the PC progressive police that some language, tasteless and prejudiced though it may be, should be squelched. My point in citing Letterman, Maher and others is to illustrate the abject hypocrisy exhibited by progressives when they give a pass to those whom they believe help to foment their revolution and castigate those who stand in opposition to their revolutionary goals.

When Herman Cain was leading in the polls in his run for the 2012 Republican nomination for President of the United States, comedienne and social commentator Janine Garofolo said this about Mr. Cain's supporters:

> "Herman Cain is probably well liked by some of the Republicans because it hides the racist elements of the Republican party, conservative movement and tea party movement, one in the same. People like Karl Rove liked to keep the racism very covert. And so Herman Cain provides this great opportunity say you can say 'Look, this is not a racist, anti-immigrant, anti-female, anti-gay movement. Look we have a Black man."

It is an empirical fact that White Republican primary voters, for several weeks, chose Herman Cain to represent their party in the 2012 Presidential election. Cain's alleged "womanizing" eventually ruined his chances to become the party's nominee.

Ms. Garofolo's hypothesis relies upon Herman Cain being a "token Black." Implied in her analysis is that Mr. Cain would have never been allowed to become the Republican party's nominee by doctrinaire party leaders, like Karl Rove, because he was a Black man.

To test Ms. Garofolo's hypothesis we looked at the voting behavior of Whites in the 2008 presidential election. The data tend to discredit Ms. Garafolo's hypothesis.

If Ms. Garofolo was right in regard to Herman Cain, imagine how powerful those forces would be in the 2008 presidential election. Despite this dynamic, Mr. Obama won the largest percentage of White support for a Democrat since 1976. He garnered 43% of the overall White vote.

Fifty-four percent of young White voters supported Mr. Obama. Among working class Whites, *Mr. Obama gained 40% of the vote, the same number as Al Gore earned from the same group back in 2000 and similar to Mr. Bush in both 2000 and 2004.* [134]

Blacks and Hispanics comprise only 21% of the voting public (12% and 9% respectively), with Asian/Pacific Islanders and others comprising 3% of the voting public. It is simply an

---

[134] Politico: Exit Polls, *How Obama Won*. David Paul Kuhn, November 5, 2008.

empirical fact that White people elected Mr. Obama. Unlike Herman Cain, who was one of several men and one woman vying for the Republican nomination, Barack Obama was the Democratic nominee for president. He could not be a token candidate by definition.

The most critical pseudo study of non-Black voting behavior in 2008 found that Mr. Obama's race cost him 3 to 5 percentage points. Another way to look at those data, unreliable as they may be, is to say that the number of White, Hispanic and other voters who withheld their vote for Mr. Obama because of his race, accounted for only 3 to 5 percentage points. But since Mr. Obama received virtually the same percentage of White votes as Al Gore in 2000 and almost identical to Mr. Bush in 2000 and 2004, it is illogical to conclude that Mr. Obama's race had any effect, other than a positive one, on his run for the White House.

Compare the above data with the fact that 96% + of Blacks voted for Mr. Obama. How many Blacks supported Mr. Obama over Hillary Clinton because he, like they, were Black? What these data suggest is that time and time again we see a selective focus by progressives that ignore the fact that choosing or not choosing a candidate because of his race is, by definition, racism, but only when it is the White voter who is put under the microscope. Ms. Garofolo projected from her own progressive infected psyche a racist element in the fact that Whites supported Mr. Cain to be the Republican nominee, choosing him for a time, before his personal troubles overwhelmed his candidacy, over 5 other White men and one White woman.

Despite the incontrovertible fact that White people elected Mr. Obama to the highest office in the land, should one criticize President Obama's policies, the Scarlett Letter of "Racist" is immediately attached to the critic of the President. If you are a Black man or woman, and you criticize Mr. Obama, you run the risk of being labeled an "Uncle Tom" or worse. If you are a White man or woman and you criticize President Obama, you run the risk of being labeled a "Racist".

It became clear by mid-way through President Obama's first term that progressives were intent upon attaching a Scarlett Letter with racial overtones to anyone who would dare criticize the President or his policies. Whereas some presidents have been blessed with a "Teflon" quality, mostly because of their charming personalities, e.g., Ronald Reagan, Bill Clinton, President Obama's racial makeup makes criticism "off limits" no matter who makes the criticism or how thoughtful and circumspect that criticism may be.

Supreme Court Justice Clarence Thomas did not enjoy these same racial benefits. Justice Thomas was subjected to, as he described it during his confirmation hearing before The Senate

Judiciary Committee, a "high tech lynching." It is not a coincidence that Justice Thomas holds beliefs that are anathema to the progressive virus's mandate.

Justice Sotomayor, on the other hand, is a darling of the progressive movement. Here is what she said before being nominated by President Obama to serve on the Supreme Court:

> "[I] would hope a "wise Latina" would make better decisions because of her life experiences than a white male."

Justice Sotomayor was given a pass for this obvious racist and sexist comment by progressives because their insistence upon equilibrium is selective. In fact, and as we see demonstrated time and time again,

> Progressives could not care less about fairness or the PC subjects they rally around. Rather, they use Scarlett Letters to label anyone who poses a threat to their dogma, but give passes to those who support their views.

Just ask yourself this question: What do you think progressives would have done if a White female nominee for the Supreme Court said this:

> "I would hope a wise White woman would make better decisions because of her life experiences than a Latina."

The ease with which this "matter" was disposed of by the progressive infected media was remarkable. Justice Sotomayor's comments about "wise Latinas" are deeply rooted and betray her prejudiced feelings and thoughts about white men. Her words were not merely a "slip of the tongue," or an ill-conceived thought. Rather, as a lifelong progressive activist she must possess animus toward the Anglo-European men who founded this country because their values, though ironically responsible in large measure for her appointment to the Supreme Court, must be undermined because of their values.

When is the last time you saw or heard anything coming from Bill Cosby? Bill is not just getting older and taking it easy. Bill is a Black man who was one of the first to break the color barrier on television. He co-starred with Robert Culp in "I spy," had his own No. 1 television comedy entitled the "Cosby Show." Bill was a brilliant stand-up comedian, who was especially gifted considering that Bill never worked "blue." He also had a pretty good film career. Bill also earned his Ed.D. from Temple University. So where is Bill Cosby?

Progressives have ostracized Bill for posing a threat to their rigid dogma. Cosby said this in the summer of 2004 when he spoke to members of Rainbow/PUSH at their annual convention:

"Your dirty laundry gets out of school at 2:30 every day, it's cursing and calling each other [the N-word] as they're walking up and down the street. They think they're hip. They can't read. They can't write. They're laughing and giggling, and they're going nowhere."

He continued:

"[B]lacks cannot simply blame Whites for problems such as high rates of teen pregnancy and school dropout. For me there is a time . . . when we have to turn the mirror around. Because for me it's almost analgesic to talk about what the white man is doing against us. And it keeps a person frozen in their seat. It keeps you frozen in your hole you're sitting in."

Cosby said he spoke out because dropout, illiteracy and teen pregnancy rates are at "epidemic" levels among less-affluent African Americans. [135]

The progressive virus abhors values and personal responsibility in the same way a bacterial infection hates antibiotics. Cosby dared to say that something is wrong in the Black community and that blaming external factors hasn't up till

---

[135] Washington Post. Debate Continues as Cosby Again Criticizes Black Youths. By Hamil R. Harris and Paul Farhi, July 3, 2004.

now and will never solve the problem. How dare he assert that something is wrong. To say that something is wrong is a value judgment. And we all know that among progressives, values are merely social constructs created for the benefit of the haves at the expense of the have-nots. How dare he assert that parents must take responsibility and children must change their self-destructive behavior.

Those infected with the progressive virus were quick to scream bloody murder. Russell Simmons, a music mogul and multi-millionaire said this:

> "[P]ointing the finger may not be helpful – we
> still have more struggle as a society and more
> work to do to reform it. "

He rejected the notion that hip-hop music has had a coarsening effect, saying

> "It is the soundtrack that reflects the struggle" of
> young people today." [136]

Notice that Simmons parroted progressive dogma when he focused on "society" and that society needed to be reformed. The externalization and displacment of responsibility are hallmark symptoms of the progressive virus.

Al Sharpton, like Simmons, recoiled over Cosby's call for personal responsibility:

---

[136] Ibid.

"But we also must be careful not to relieve the general community of what they've done to our community." [137]

Sharpton and Simmons are relatively high profile personalities. Sharpton has a gig on MSNBC and Simmons is still working to sell young Blacks his products, including credit cards, and making millions doing it. But where is the very talented Bill Cosby? Cosby is still there, but those who control access to the media, those same people severely infected with the progressive virus, have limited Bill Cosby's access to the American public. He is too much of a threat.

Anti-progressives should exercise caution when condemning tasteless or prejudiced speech. Describing such speech in negative terms is one thing, but calling for the firing of individuals who exhibit such behavior or other coercive pressure applied by groups, must be avoided. Progressives need to control speech to effectuate their revolution. This has been the pattern in every single progressive, socialist, Marxist revolution on record. By joining progressives in the quelling of free speech, even when the proverbial shoe is on the other foot, accedes to progressive's revolutionary ambitions.

---

[137] Ibid.

CHAPTER FIFTEEN

The Perfect Face

A CRITICALLY IMPORTANT POINT to make when analyzing the progressive virus's modus operandi is the fact that the progressive virus can only survive when shrouded within a non-threatening façade or when the virus works out of the light of day.

In America and elsewhere that façade is seen clearly in the progressive's choice of "issues" in need of social justice. We have chronicled the progressive's handiwork in how they infiltrate governmental agencies, unions and program those who teach our children. Still, the virus cannot achieve all of its work in absolute stealth mode. The virus needs a face, a front man.

The progressive's front man would ideally possess characteristics that make it virtually impossible to strip away his façade. He should be someone so insulated that when attempts are made to strip away the façade, the mere act of trying to expose the front man's true nature is forbidden. The front man should be warm, charming, have a beautiful voice and possess a "million dollar smile." The progressive's front man would ideally have a family that is attractive and be someone who possesses wit and humor. He should be smart and well educated.

The ideal front man would possess some inherent characteristic that would make it virtually impossible for anyone to criticize him or his policies without the critic's motives being brought into question. He should be patient, low-key, no drama and above all else, willing to tow the line of those progressives who put him into power.

Progressives need to know that they can control their front man, because they will recognize that anyone so charming, warm and attractive could stray from the program they have designed for him. Ideally, the front man would be vulnerable to blackmail if he should stray from the progressive program.

The choice of an ideal front man will require that he possesses relatively little experience in politics. The less history, the less explaining. Such a front man will appear to come out of nowhere. This is because his selection was made based upon his personal qualities as a front man, not political leader. Like a made up musical group whose members are chosen by producers because they look like teen idols, the fact that they can't play a musical instrument is of little consequence. They only have to look and act the part.

When I was a child we played a game we called "hide the thimble." The most interesting thing about the game was that the thimble had to be "hidden" in plain view. In that respect it was a game that tested the player's ability to use "figure/ground" cloaking. We see this with wildlife that are masters at blending into the background.

The front man's public agenda will be eerily similar to a game of hide the thimble. His legislative efforts and related causes will be hidden in plain sight. A social justice mantle will protect his public agenda. His agenda will benefit from a halo effect wherein his own personal charm and attractiveness will give credibility to his agenda. Stripping away the façade will be perceived as an assault on social justice.

The front man will elicit the psychological mechanism of projection. People from all walks of life will project upon the front man a primitive idealization. They will project upon this one man all of their hopes and dreams and childlike trust. In that respect, the front man will be like a movie star upon whom his adoring fans project qualities and powers that comport with the roles he plays and not the true nature of the man.

One will be able to recognize the existence of a front man by the fact that there will be some aspects of his life that will be mysteriously "missing" or there will be gaps in his personal history. These "gaps" in background are tells that even though the front man is good, he is not perfect. Those who chose him have deleted those parts of his history that would expose his true nature. Nevertheless, the front man's charm and attractiveness will make it very difficult for others to investigate his past because the very act of doing so will result in being eviscerated in the public square by the front man's sycophants.

Another "tell" that informs that one is dealing with a front man, can be ascertained by his past associations. Because the front man will be recruited after his progressive bona fides are formed, his early life and that time leading up to his anointing as the front man will reveal his true colors.

Look closely at who he looked up to and to whom he admired during his developmental years. Study closely his early education and look closely at the lives and background of those people. Strip away the façade and you will find revolutionaries.

The revolutionaries will have a history of anarchist and/or a terrorist past. The front man's associations will be disproportionately comprised of former members of revolutionary groups who were active in the 1960's. These progressive revolutionaries will have made the transition from the despair of terrorism and anarchy to the Marxist activist whose plan is to subvert the "system" then take it over from within. Thus, the front man is one of their most important tools to subvert their enemies.

Another tell will be evident by how the front man's sycophants jump in to help him when any attempt is made to strip away his façade. For instance, the mere mention of the front man's associations with Marxist revolutionaries will engender an immediate and energized attempt to stifle and shroud such efforts. Should that fail, every excuse imaginable will be put into action to minimize, negate or deny that any association with revolutionaries ever existed. "I smoked but I did not inhale" will be the operant metaphor when exposing the front man's association with revolutionaries.

Another tell will be evinced by how suspiciously inept the front man will be vetted. The front man's opponents will be vetted with a fine-toothed comb. Every last detail of his opponent's life will be excised and put under the microscope. But when it comes to the front man, behavior that would automatically qualify as perfect fodder for the press will be mysteriously shrouded or disappear.

The ideal front man would not possess a characteristic that would, by law, disqualify him. However, if the front man is so charming, so attractive and so available and willing, progressive revolutionaries will search for the front man's fatal flaw to insure that he remains supplicant.

The front man's election opponents will exhibit frustration and amazement that such a candidate may defeat them.

Depending upon the political power of the front man's opponent, another tell will manifest in how his opponent will attempt to send thinly veiled messages to the voting public. These messages allude to his true nature without ever coming out and saying it. The front man's opponent will understand who he is and will be conflicted over their desire to attack him. If the front man's opponent is a progressive or progressive sympathizer, usually their compliance can be bought.

The perfect environment for the appearance of the ideal front man is one in which the country finds itself in decline. The front man's predecessor will, in many ways, be the polar opposite of him. Where the front man is articulate, his ideal predecessor would have been inarticulate. Whereas the front man will make Americans feel good about their president, his predecessor would have engendered embarrassment, especially among liberals. It is within an environment of economic and cultural discontent that will set the stage for the front man's appearance. The progressives will see their once in a generation chance to pounce.

The front man's power and influence will grow less persuasive as time passes. This phenomenon is not merely related to the man, although that, too, but because over time the public grows weary of the same expressions of charm. Although not absolutely necessary, it is likely that the front man will have tendencies toward narcissism. This means that his pleasure with himself and his belief that he is the most charming and intelligent person in the room, wears thin as time passes.

Another reason the front man's influence wanes over time is that so many ideals are projected upon him, no man can live up to his constituents dreams. At first the front man's "failures" will be blamed on his opponents, but over time, the front man will disappoint his sycophant's unrealistic dreams and projections and because of his position of power he will be blamed.

Progressives know that their front man has a shelf life. Thus, one can expect a massive push to change the DNA of America right out of the box. The Marxist revolutionaries believe that if their front man is successful they can make so many changes to the very soul of America that they will have sowed the seeds of its destruction.

Should the re-election of their front man be in jeopardy, you can look forward to some cataclysmic event that will insure his re-election. That cataclysmic event is likely to involve a foreign adventure that will encourage the public to rally around the front man. Once in power, the progressives will not go quietly.

CHAPTER SIXTEEN

Disassembling the Progressive Virus

Shrouded Groups

THE PROGRESSIVE VIRUS'S DNA must remain encased in a protective non-threatening envelope in order to survive. In that respect, it functions exactly like a biological virus.

Take for instance the bacteriophage virus. The bacteriophage begins its attack by coming into contact with its victim, a bacterial cell. It perforates (lyses) the cell wall of the bacterium and injects its virus DNA into its victim. It does not take long before the victim's DNA manufacturing facility is commandeered by the virus. Once the virus takes control, the bacterium victim begins to make virus DNA, not its own DNA. It continues making virus DNA until it bursts (this causes its death) and releases a million more virus particles to repeat the process.

The façade used by progressives is designed to hide their true nature from those who are being asked to accede their power to them. Progressives come across as nice liberals who are only trying to do good for society. This is ironic because progressives do not believe in "good" as an objective concept.

Progressives know that if the population at large really understood what they were up to, Americans would recoil at their true nature. Take, for example, Van Jones:

> "Jones' new approach was modeled on the tactics outlined by the famed radical organizer Saul Alinsky, who stressed the need for revolutionaries to **mask the extremism of their objectives** and to present themselves as moderates until they could gain some control over the machinery of political power. In a 2005 interview, Jones stated that he still considered himself a revolutionary, but a more effective one thanks to his revised tactics."
>
> (Emphasis added) [138]

After 25 years of studying the progressive virus and those who carry it, I have found that if you strip away the protective shroud worn by progressives, what you find are men and women dedicated to taking the reins of government, then increasing the power and scope of governmental power. Once in charge, progressives will use their power to wield totalitarian dominance over their fellow citizens. We find men and women who are angry and who are intent upon fomenting a revolution that is specifically designed to destroy free will and confiscate, then redistribute, wealth. Once progressives destroy free will

---

[138] Discover the Networks: A Guide to the Political Left. March, 2012.

and institute tyranny, they are intent upon becoming the totalitarian rulers of the world. This description of progressives may sound "over the top," but the progressive virus, like the bacteriophage, won't stop until it kills its victim.

Progressives are notoriously passive aggressive and psychologically sophisticated. They are masters at using psychological triggers to get what they want. They are, without exception, agnostic or atheist. They have sublimated their violent tendencies and have learned to become pleasant and soft-spoken.

The men are non-threatening for the most part, often appearing to be gender amorphous. Many are vegetarian and involved in animal rights, but do not love animals, per se. For example, progressives may belong to PETA, but they would be less likely to volunteer at an animal rescue shelter or take into their home stray animals.

Trace the history of many a progressive activist and you will find, if you go back in time, an anarchist who once terrorized his or her way through life. Whether it was the "Weathermen" or The Students for a Democratic Society (SDS) or the Black Panthers, these groups were the breeding grounds where the non-threatening progressives of today got their start.

Those infected with the progressive virus are not individualists. They work in groups. Progressives start and belong to groups named to appear to be wholesome and non-threatening. The sheer number of progressive groups using shrouded names is very telling. The following CATEGORY listing of progressive groups is striking. Realize that each CATEGORY includes several specific organizations each with its own progressive agenda, funding, purpose and non-threatening name:

1.0 Progressive Electoral Politics Organizations

1.1. Progressive Political Parties

1.2. Progressive State and Local Legislation Groups

1.3. Progressive Lobbying and Electoral Action Groups

1.4. Progressive Democratic Party Election Groups

1.5. Progressive Voter Engagement Groups

1.6. Election Reform Groups

1.7. Government Accountability Groups

2. Peace and U.S. Foreign Policy Organizations

2.1. Coalitions of Peace Groups

2.2. General Peace Groups

2.3. Veterans Peace Groups

2.4. Women's Peace Groups

2.5. Student Peace Groups

2.6. Nuclear Weapons-Focused Groups

2.7. Peace Building Groups

2.8. Conscientious Objection to War Groups

2.9. Religious Peace Groups

2.10. Nonviolent Peacemaker Groups

2.11. Nonviolent Action Policy Groups

2.12. Other Specialized Peace Groups

2.13. Peace Policy Institutes

3. International Justice Organizations

3.1. International Human Rights Groups

3.2. Regional Human Rights Groups

3.3. International Economic Justice Groups

3.4. International Development Groups

4. Economic Justice Organizations

4.1. Worker Justice and Democracy Groups

4.2. International Worker Justice and Democracy Groups

4.3. Anti-Poverty and Low Income Housing Groups

4.4. Anti-Poverty Policy Groups

4.5. Employment Groups

4.6. Economic Justice Groups

4.7. Anti-Corporate Domination Groups

4.8. Progressive Economic Research Groups

4.9. Progressive Tax Groups

4.10. Consumer Protection Groups

4.11. Socially Responsible Business Groups

4.12. Worker Ownership Groups

5. Civil Liberties Organizations

5.1. Civil Liberties Groups

5.2. Electronic Privacy Groups

5.3. Freedom of Religion Groups

6. Social Justice Organizations

6.1. Civil Rights Groups

6.2. Civil Rights Constituency Groups

6.3. Legal Defense of Civil Rights Groups

6.4. Immigration Rights Groups

6.5. Criminal Justice Groups

6.6. Groups Challenging Capital Punishment

6.7. Community Organizing Groups

6.8. Disability Rights Groups

6.9. Elder Advocacy Groups

6.10. Children Advocacy Groups

6.11. Family Advocacy Groups

6.12. Feminist / Women's Liberation Groups

6.13. Gay, Lesbian, Bisexual, and Transgender Liberation Groups

6.14. Family Planning Groups

7. Health Advocacy Organizations

7.1. Healthcare Advocacy Groups

7.2. Anti-Smoking Groups

8. Environmental Organizations

8.1. Broad-Focus Environmental Groups

11.4. Progressive Lawyer Groups

11.5. Progressive Scientist Groups

11.6. Other Progressive Professional Groups

12. Progressive Infrastructure Organizations

12.1. General Progressive Policy Groups

12.2. General Legal Support Groups

12.3. Progressive Foundations

12.4. Progressive Groups Monitoring Foundations

12.5. Other Progressive Support Groups [139]

Since progressives operate within and are dependent upon groups, it is important to understand the nature of group psychology. Groups invariably take on characteristics that are not merely the sum of their parts. Groups may be made up of individuals, but once the group forms, its takes on a life of its own.

People do things in groups that they would never do as individuals. For instance, those inclined not to fight or be confrontational have no problem doing those things when part of a group. Gangs illustrate this behavior most graphically. However, any group with plenary power, and this would include

---

[139] For a complete listing of the individual groups in each CATEGORY, Visit this website: http://www.startguide.org/orgs/orgs00.html

all governmental agencies and bureaucracies, behave exactly like gangs.

Survival within an organization is different than an individual surviving in the culture at large. Groups, especially governmental groups, survive long after they have lost any semblance of positive purpose. Governmental groups are so autonomous, that when they are proven to cause more harm than good, they are funded and continue their assault upon those whom they regulate. Individuals do not benefit from this disconnect between merit and survival.

For example, individual entrepreneurs selling a product or service necessarily subject themselves to a natural selection in the marketplace. If the entrepreneur has something people want, then he or she survives, if not, failure is inevitable. On the other hand, tenured professors are virtually "fire proof." As long as they can navigate the political waters in their university, they can virtually assure themselves a long career and generous pension.

Career union members are yet another example of how survival in a group is different than survival as an individual in the marketplace. For example, this KTLA television story highlights how unionized teachers are protected even when they commit heinous crimes against children:

"LOS ANGELES (KTLA) – An LAUSD teacher accused of molestation was allowed to return to the classroom, despite prior accusations of abuse. Paul William Chapel, 50, of Chatsworth is currently accused of molesting four children, including at least one student at Telefair Elementary School in Pacoima. Chapel is charged with 16 counts of sex abuse involving three girls and one boy, all under 14 years old." [140]

The story went on to say this:

"A major obstacle has been a clause in LAUSD teacher contracts that limits how long allegations remain in a teacher's file. Under the clause, alleged misconduct that does not result in discipline – no matter how serious – is removed from personnel files after four years. Teachers cannot be subject to punishment based on an expired file." [141]

In yet one more example of group dynamics, another teacher in the Los Angeles School District took photos of children whose mouths he duct-taped closed while placing cockroaches on their faces. This same teacher took pictures of boys and girls eating

---

[140] KTLA Television News, March 7, 2012.
[141] Ibid.

semen-covered cookies (DNA testing confirmed it was his semen). But wait, it gets worse, the teacher extorted a huge severance package from California Taxpayers because otherwise, according to union rules, he could not be fired.

> "A teacher charged with 23 counts of lewd conduct in his classroom successfully thwarted attempts by the Los Angeles Unified School District to fire him. In the process, the teacher, who is accused of spoon-feeding his semen to blindfolded children, managed to retain lifetime health-benefits provided by the nation's second-largest school system. Former Miramonte Elementary School teacher Mark Berndt also automatically receives nearly $4,000 a month in pension from the California State Teachers' Retirement System." [142]

Groups ultimately select for and reward mediocrity; whereas, when it comes to individuals, excellence is selected. Groups not only select mediocrity, they deselect excellence. It has long been known that group decision-making is fraught with any number of problems.

---

[142] Los Angeles Times, February 1, 2012.

Janis Irving coined the term "groupthink' to describe the distortions of reasoning that people in groups often make. Here are a couple of definitions of Groupthink:

- Groupthink is a type of thought exhibited by group members who try to minimize conflict and reach consensus without critically testing, analyzing, and evaluating ideas. During Groupthink, members of the group avoid promoting viewpoints outside the comfort zone of consensus thinking. A variety of motives for this may exist such as a desire to avoid being seen as foolish, or a desire to avoid embarrassing or angering other members of the group. Groupthink may cause groups to make hasty, irrational decisions, where individual doubts are set aside, for fear of upsetting the group's balance.

- Groupthink occurs in groups when individual thinking or individual creativity is lost or subverted to stay within the comfort zone of the consensus view. People's common sense and ability to perform problem solving, make good decisions, and raise unpopular views are overridden by the desire for group consensus.[143]

Progressives cannot realize their dream of totalitarian control without working in groups and then harnessing the power of government's groups, that is, government's agencies and bureaucracies. Progressives recognize that the public would shy away from their unbridled ambition, which requires centralized governmental power, if they truly understood what was happening to them. Recognizing this problem, progressives argue that governmental power is less virulent and dangerous than corporate power. Nothing could be further from the truth.

Corporations, even the worst of them, cannot break down your door at 10 A.M. in the morning and arrest you, but the government can. Corporations cannot indict, try, then convict you and sentence you to death, but the government can. The worst corporations may lie, cheat and steal, but only the government can garnish wages, put you in jail for not paying your taxes, tell you where you can live, how big your house can be, how tall your fence can be, mandate the types of light bulbs you must use, where your kids can go to school, what they will be taught, the kinds of spices you can put on your food, mandate that you be patted down at the airport, mandate that

---

[143] Janis Irving L. 1982 Groupthink: Psychological Studies of Policy Decisions and Fiascos second edition. Boston: Houghton-Mifflin.

you buy a license to open a business, even if it is a kid's lemonade stand.

Political groups comprised of progressives invariably employ Marxist and Communist strategies. Invariably they censor, regulate, stifle their opponents and, if necessary, will eventually eradicate their enemies. Progressives, when they have their way, inevitably create governments that evolve into communist or communist-like entities.

In *The Black Book of Communism: Crimes, Terror, Repression,* the authors write:

> "Revolutions, like trees, must be judged by their fruit," Ignazio Silone wrote, and this is the standard the authors apply to the Communist experience—in the China of "the Great Helmsman," Kim Il Sung's Korea, Vietnam under "Uncle Ho" and Cuba under Castro, Ethiopia under Mengistu, Angola under Neto, and Afghanistan under Najibullah. The authors, all distinguished scholars based in Europe, document Communist crimes against humanity, but also crimes against national and universal culture, from Stalin's destruction of hundreds of churches in Moscow to Ceausescu's leveling of the historic heart of Bucharest to the widescale devastation

visited on Chinese culture by Mao's Red Guards."
144

The authors provide these sobering numbers:

The total death toll of these progressive infected revolutions is over 94 million, not counting the "excess deaths" (decrease of the population due to lower than-expected birth rates).

65 million in the People's Republic of China

20 million in the Soviet Union

2 million in Cambodia

2 million in North Korea

1.7 million in Africa

1.5 million in Afghanistan

1 million in the Communist states of Eastern Europe

1 million in Vietnam

150,000 in Latin America

10,000 deaths resulting from actions of the international Communist movement and Communist parties not in power.

---

144 The Black Book of Communism: Crimes, Terror, Repression by Stéphane Courtois". Harvard University Press. Retrieved 2008-02-24.

Mass murder is the quintessential example of controlling speech. In each instance of genocide those targeted for mass extinction would not shut up.

Each totalitarian regime began as a progressive political movement, intent upon establishing social justice. "Creeping progressivism" characterizes the nascent beginning of every revolution. Each regime ultimately succumbed to the totalitarian mandate of progressivism. How does progressivism evolve into totalitarian control? When each regime's progressive PC rules no longer stifled its adversaries, those threatening the progressive virus were fired from their media job or ostracized. When that would not shut up their enemies they sent them to re-education camps. When that didn't work purveyors of threatening speech were exiled to far off lands. Ultimately, mass murder became the best and final choice to control speech and stifle threatening ideas. It is indisputable that each successful progressive revolution began with the call for and implementation of social justice. Many ended in mass murder.

One of the ploys used by the progressive virus is that it appears to be non-threatening. It chooses issues "in need of social justice" that are designed to have universal appeal. If one looks closely, however, each progressive issue is merely a means to an end. And that end is rigid control through regulation, taxation and confiscation of private wealth.

Class envy is as important to progressive revolutions as fuel is to an internal combustion engine. One group is pitted against the other, and those competing groups are typically characterized as the haves versus the have-nots. In the latest iteration in America, this false battle has been characterized as the 99% versus the 1%. By appealing to the entitlement mentality of the have-nots, progressives can foment their plan to garner the power to confiscate, then redistribute, to the have-nots. Have-nots are led to believe that they, too, will obtain the success and wealth of the haves, thanks to the largesse of the government, if only they empower progressive politicians to restore social justice. But what invariably occurs is that redistribution strips the society of excellence, and lowers the standard of living for everyone. This is why the streets of Cuba are filled with 1950s American made automobiles and Soviet bloc countries produced cars like the Yugo.

CHAPTER SEVENTEEN

Disassembling the Virus

Global Warming/Cap and Trade

ONE SUCH EXAMPLE OF a progressive issue tailor made for a good dose of social justice is Cap and Trade, a method by which CO_2 emissions, among other so-called greenhouse gases, will purportedly be reduced. Ultimately, Cap and Trade seeks to regulate carbon, and if you regulate carbon, you control life itself. And why should carbon be regulated? Global Warming. John Griffing, writing for the American Thinker, wrote this about Cap and Trade:

> "Masquerading as an instrument of environmental salvation, the Waxman-Markey cap-and-trade bill will result in one of the largest seizures of wealth in human history. The legislation will wreak havoc on American manufacturing and industry, and coerce the conformity of an already economically squeezed populace. The bill is a transparent power grab,

based on a fictional crisis-the left's ever-dependable threat of global warming.

But global warming is finally coming under the scrutiny it deserves. Not only are NASA satellites showing a cooling trend, but 700 scientists - to the UN's 50 - have come out in opposition to the patently false claims of the global warming lobby. Most damning, Harvard meteorologists have been unable to replicate the findings of the UN's International Panel on Climate Change (IPCC) without the use of a technique called "data-padding. [145] The IPCC actually admitted to engaging in this deceptive practice. Without this padding, the infamous warming trend falls by several degrees. In essence, the IPCC and its primary source manipulated data (dare we say "lied"?) to produce a desired result. [146]

Notwithstanding the condescending treatment of those who would dare to assert that global warming science is more complex than a politician's slide show that looks at only a sliver of data, the issue *is* much more complex and nuanced.

---

[145] Willie H. Soon, David R. Legates, and Sallie L. Baliunas, "Estimation and representation of long-term (>40 year) trends of Northern-Hemisphere-gridded surface temperature: A note of caution," Geophysical Research Letters, vol. 31, 14 February 2004, 2.

[146] American Thinker. Cap and Trade: The Big Con. John Griffing, July 3, 2009.

Thoughtful analysis suggests that something else is afoot. None other than the Commerce's Department National Climatic Data Center, published these facts:

"[A]nother climate mystery that scientists have puzzled over in recent years is why during the "middle Holocene" (roughly 7,000 to 5,000 years ago), **temperatures seemed to be warmer than even present day temperatures**. Indeed, some of the paleoclimatic data suggest that temperatures were several degrees Celsius hotter than today (2004). With the growing concern about the potential for global warming, such information is of great interest to climate scientists. It now appears that temperatures were generally warmer, but only in the summer in the northern hemisphere. **The cause? Changes in the Earth's orbit that operate slowly over thousands and millions of years that change the amount of solar radiation reaching each latitudinal band of the Earth during each month.** (See The Ice Age online slide set and Climate Science 100,000 Years for more on orbital forcing.) Such orbital changes can be calculated, and what they indicate is that the northern hemisphere should have been warmer in the summer and colder in the winter than at present during the mid-Holocene. [147]

When confronted with these data progressive apologists reflexively retort that 97% of climate scientists agree that the Earth is warming. Those data citing the 97% figure come from a study: Doran, P. T. and M. Kendall Zimmerman (2009), *Examining the Scientific Consensus on Climate Change*, Eos Trans. AGU, 90. It is never mentioned that the scientists who were chosen to sample were self-selected. How many scientists were surveyed? 79.

According to Popular Technology Net, 900 peer reviewed research studies are skeptical of the alarms raised by global warming scientists. The following climate scientists are not convinced that man is the significant factor involved in climate change:

- *"I'm sure the majority (but not all) of my IPCC colleagues cringe when I say this, but I see neither the developing catastrophe nor the smoking gun proving that human activity is to blame for most of the warming we see."* – John R. Christy

John R. Christy, B.A. Mathematics, California State University (1973), M.S. Atmospheric Science, University of Illinois (1984),

---

[147] Commerce Department of the United States. National Clmatic Data Center. National Environmental, Satelite and Data Center. NOAA. *Paleoclimatology.*

Ph.D. Atmospheric Science, University of Illinois (1987), NASA Exceptional Scientific Achievement Medal (1991), American Meteorological Society's Special Award (1996), Member, Committee on Earth Studies, Space Studies Board (1998-2001), Alabama State Climatologist (2000-Present), Fellow, American Meteorological Society (2002), Panel Member, Official Statement on Climate Change, American Geophysical Union (2003), Member, Committee on Environmental Satellite Data Utilization, Space Studies Board (2003-2004), Member, Committee on Surface Temperature Reconstructions for the last 2,000 years, National Research Council (2006), Distinguished Professor of Atmospheric Science, University of Alabama in Huntsville (1991-Present), Director of the Earth System Science Center, University of Alabama in Huntsville (2000-Present), Contributor, IPCC (1992, 1994, 1996, 2007), Lead Author, IPCC (2001)

- *"A number of studies point to sources other than greenhouse gases as explanations for the modest warming trend of the late 20th century." –* Patrick J. Michaels

Patrick J. Michaels, A.B. Biological Sciences, University of Chicago (1971), S.M. Biology, University of Chicago (1975), Ph.D. Ecological Climatology, University of Wisconsin-Madison (1979), Research and Project Assistant, Center for Climatic Research, University of Wisconsin (1976-1979), Assistant Professor of Environmental Sciences, University of Virginia (1980-1986), Virginia State Climatologist (1980-2007), President, Central Virginia Chapter, American Meteorological Society (1986-1987), Executive Board, American Association of State Climatologists (1986-1989), Associate Professor of Environmental Sciences, University of Virginia (1986-1995), President, American Association of State Climatologists (1987-1988), Chair, Committee on Applied Climatology, American Meteorological Society (1988-1999), Senior Fellow in Environmental Studies,

ANTHONY NAPOLEON

Cato Institute (1992-Present), Visiting Scientist, Marshall Institute (1996-Present), Member, American Association for the Advancement of Science, Member, Association of American Geographers, Member, Sigma Xi, The Scientific Research Society, Professor of Environmental Sciences, University of Virginia (1996-Present), Contributor and Expert Reviewer, IPCC (1990, 1992, 1995, 2001, 2007)

- *"Given that the evidence strongly implies that anthropogenic warming has been greatly exaggerated, the basis for alarm due to such warming is similarly diminished."* – Richard S. Lindzen

Richard S. Lindzen, A.B. Physics *Magna Cum Laude*, Harvard University (1960), S.M. Applied Mathematics, Harvard University (1961), Ph.D. Applied Mathematics, Harvard University (1964), Research Associate in Meteorology, University of Washington (1964-1965), NATO Post-Doctoral Fellow at the Institute for Theoretical Meteorology, University of Oslo (1965-1966), Research Scientist, National Center for Atmospheric Research (1966-1967), Visiting Lecturer in Meteorology, UCLA (1967), NCAR Outstanding Publication Award (1967), AMS Meisinger Award (1968), Associate Professor and Professor of Meteorology, University of Chicago (1968-1972), Summer Lecturer, NCAR Colloquium (1968, 1972, 1978), AGU Macelwane Award (1969), Visiting Professor, Department of Environmental Sciences, Tel Aviv University (1969), Alfred P. Sloan Fellowship (1970-1976), Gordon McKay Professor of Dynamic Meteorology, Harvard University (1972-1983), Visiting Professor of Dynamic Meteorology, Massachusetts Institute of Technology (1975), Lady Davis Visiting Professor, Department of Meteorology, The Hebrew University (1979), Director, Center for Earth and Planetary Physics, Harvard University (1980-1983), Robert P. Burden Professor of Dynamical Meteorology, Harvard University (1982-1983), AMS Charney Award (1985), Vikram Amblal Sarabhai Professor, Physical Research Laboratory, Ahmedabad,

India (1985), Japanese Society for the Promotion of Science Fellowship (1986-1987), Distinguished Visiting Scientist, Jet Propulsion Laboratory, NASA (1988-Present), Sackler Visiting Professor, Tel Aviv University (1992), Landsdowne Lecturer, University of Victoria (1993), Bernhard Haurwitz Memorial Lecturer, American Meteorological Society (1997), Fellow, American Academy of Arts & Sciences; Fellow, American Association for the Advancement of Science; Fellow, American Geophysical Union; Fellow, American Meteorological Society; Member, Norwegian Academy of Science and Letters; Member, Sigma Xi, The Scientific Research Society; Member, National Academy of Sciences; ISI Highly Cited Researcher; Alfred P. Sloan Professor of Meteorology, Department of Earth, Atmospheric and Planetary Sciences, Massachusetts Institute of Technology (1983-Present), Lead Author, IPCC (2001)

- *"As a climate researcher, I am increasingly convinced that most of our recent global warming has been natural, not manmade."* – Roy W. Spencer

Roy W. Spencer, B.S. Atmospheric Sciences, University of Michigan (1978), M.S. Meteorology, University of Wisconsin (1980), Ph.D. Meteorology, University of Wisconsin (1982), Research Scientist, Space Science and Engineering Center, University of Wisconsin (1982-1984), Senior Scientist for Climate Studies, Marshall Space Flight Center, NASA (1984-2001), MSFC Center Director's Commendation (1989), NASA Exceptional Scientific Achievement Medal (1991), U.S. Team Leader, Multichannel Imaging Microwave Radiometer (MIMR) Team, NASA (1992-Present), Team Leader, AMSR-E Science Team, NASA (1994-Present), American Meteorological Society's Special Award (1996), Principal Research Scientist, Earth System Science Center, University of Alabama in Huntsville (2001-Present)

- *"We see no evidence in the climate record that the increase in CO2, which is real, has any appreciable effect on the global temperature."* – S. Fred Singer

S. Fred Singer, BEE, Ohio State University (1943), A.M. Physics, Princeton University (1944), Ph.D. Physics, Princeton University (1948), Research Physicist, Upper Atmosphere Rocket Program, Applied Physics Laboratory, Johns Hopkins University (1946-1950), Scientific Liaison Officer, U.S. Office of Naval Research (1950-1953), Director, Center for Atmospheric and Space Physics, and Professor of Physics, University of Maryland (1953-1962), White House Commendation for Early Design of Space Satellites (1954), Visiting Scientist, Jet Propulsion Laboratory, Cal Tech (1961-1962), First Director, National Weather Satellite Center (1962-1964), First Dean of the School of Environmental and Planetary Sciences, University of Miami (1964-1967), Deputy Assistant Secretary (Water Quality and Research), U.S. Department of the Interior (1967-1970), Deputy Assistant Administrator, U.S. Environmental Protection Agency (1970-1971), Federal Executive Fellow, The Brookings Institution (1971), Professor of Environmental Science, University of Virginia (1971-1994), U.S. National Academy of Sciences Exchange Scholar, Soviet Academy of Sciences Institute for Physics of the Earth (1972), Member, Governor of Virginia Task Force on Transportation (1975), First Sid Richardson Professor, Lyndon Baines Johnson School for Public Affairs, University of Texas (1978), Vice Chairman and Member, National Advisory Committee on Oceans and Atmospheres (1981-1986), Senior Fellow, The Heritage Foundation (1982-1983), Member, U.S. Department of State Science Advisory Board (Oceans, Environment, Science) (1982-1987), Member, Acid Rain Panel, White House Office of Science and Technology Policy (1982-1987), Member, NASA Space Applications Advisory Committee (1983-1985), Member, U.S. Department of Energy Nuclear Waste Panel (1984), Visiting Eminent Scholar, George Mason University (1984-1987), Chief Scientist, U.S. Department of

Transportation (1987-1989), Member, White House Panel on U.S.-Brazil Science and Technology Exchange (1987), Distinguished Research Professor, Institute for Space Science and Technology (1989-1994), Guest Scholar, Woodrow Wilson International Center for Scholars, Smithsonian Institute (1991), Guest Scholar, National Air and Space Museum, Smithsonian Institute (1991), Distinguished Visiting Fellow, The Hoover Institution, Stanford University (1992-1993), Distinguished Research Professor, Institute for Humane Studies, George Mason University (1994-2000), Commendation for Research on Particle Clouds, NASA (1997), Research Fellow, Independent Institute (1997), Director and President, The Science and Environmental Policy Project (1989-Present), Expert Reviewer, IPCC (2001)

- *"I find no compelling reason to believe that the earth will necessarily experience any global warming as a consequence of the ongoing rise in the atmosphere's carbon dioxide concentration."* – Sherwood B. Idso

Sherwood B. Idso, B.S. Physics *Cum Laude*, University of Minnesota (1964), M.S. Soil Science, University of Minnesota (1966), Ph.D. Soil Science, University of Minnesota (1967), Research Assistant in Physics, University of Minnesota (1962), National Defense Education Act Fellowship (1964-1967), Research Soil Scientist, U.S. Water Conservation Laboratory, Agricultural Research Service, U.S. Department of Agriculture (1967-1974), Editorial Board Member, Agricultural and Forest Meteorology Journal (1972-1993), Secretary, American Meteorological Society, Central Arizona Chapter (1973-1974), Vice-Chair, American Meteorological Society, Central Arizona Chapter (1974-1975), Research Physicist, U.S. Water Conservation Laboratory, Agricultural Research Service, U.S. Department of Agriculture (1974-2001), Chair, American Meteorological Society, Central Arizona Chapter (1975-1976), Arthur S. Flemming Award (1977), Secretary, Sigma Xi – The

Research Society, Arizona State University Chapter (1979-1980), President, Sigma Xi – The Research Society, Arizona State University Chapter (1980-1982), Member, Task Force on "Alternative Crops", Council for Agricultural Science and Technology (1983), Adjunct Professor of Geography and Plant Biology, Arizona State University (1984-2007), Editorial Board Member, Environmental and Experimental Botany Journal (1993-Present), Member, Botanical Society of America; Member, American Geophysical Union; Member, American Society of Agronomy; ISI Highly Cited Researcher; President, Center for the Study of Carbon Dioxide and Global Change (2001-Present) [148]

The mistake that anti-progressives make when they criticize the global warming lobby is that they imply, through their words, and sometimes their actions, that raping and pillaging the environment is "just fine."

The earth goes through cycles of heating and cooling. Nevertheless, it is unreasonable to assert that man's behavior has absolutely nothing to do with temperature fluctuations. Regardless, it is the attitude of some anti-progressives that implies it's OK to pay little or no attention to real pollutants, including some greenhouse gases, that helps progressives in their push to invoke a Cap and Trade mandate that buys them power.

---

[148] Popular Technology. September 25, 2010.

CHAPTER EIGHTEEN

Disassembling the Virus

The Patient Protection and Affordable Care Act

THE PATIENT PROTECTION AND Affordable Care Act is over 2000 pages long. No one in the Congress or Senate read the entire 2000 pages before they voted, in part, because Speaker of the House Nancy Pelosi ram-rodded the bill through the review process and said that:

> "Congress would have to pass the bill in order to find out what's in it." [149]

Throughout the debate in both the Senate and House, the number of uninsured in the United States was represented to be staggeringly high. Some legislators saying that the figure approached nearly 50 million people. But was that true?

> "In October of 2008 The Kaiser Commission released a report on the demographics of the reputed 45 million United States citizens who allegedly have no health insurance. It turns out

---

[149] Nancy Pelosi, speaking to: Legislative Conference for the National Association of Counties, March 3, 2009.

that the number of those who actually can't afford that coverage is significantly smaller. Of the 311 million persons who make up the US population 53% receive employer sponsored health insurance, 14% are on Medicare, 13% on Medicaid and 5% purchase their own health insurance coverage. That leaves 15% of the 311 million who represent the uninsured ranks, or 46.5 million people. However, looking further at the uninsured we find that 69% are members of a family where one or more of the members are working full time, 12% are in part time employment and 19% have no family members working at all; the latter figure represents less than 9 million people.

In 2012 the Federal Poverty Level (FPL) for a family of four was $23,050 of annual income. In 2010 15.1% of Americans (47 million) lived in poverty. On the other hand 16.3% (51 million) of US citizens were without health insurance in 2010. Three groups of people made up the bulk of that latter number; foreign-born residents who are not US citizens, young adults aged 18 to 25 and low-income families with less than $24,000 worth of annual income. On the other hand, the children of the latter group aged 18 and under would qualify for the State Children's Health Insurance Plan (SCHIP) and those numbers amount to 20% of all uninsured persons or 10.2 million people. Those folks in the 19 to 25 age bracket are uninsured because they have chosen to spend their money on a variety of other more pleasurable pursuits. At the present time however, no person is ever deprived of healthcare regardless of their place in the socio-economic strata. I currently provide primary care at a Healthcare clinic in Warren Ohio, one of four such establishments within a 20 mile radius, where people on Medicare, Medicaid, the uninsured but employed, and the non-working uninsured are cared for. (Note: A period should follow the word "for", yes?)We also treat a small number of persons who do have private health insurance. The uninsured employed pay for their visits on a sliding scale determined by their 1040 IRS form from the previous year. Many of those uninsured persons, whether they have a job or not, have been referred to us for follow-up from a local emergency room where they were treated and admitted (at no expense to them) or treated and released. No sick person, regardless of age, gender, work status or insurability is denied access to care in our nation. Those who say otherwise are simply either ignorant of the facts or they willingly lie. [150]

Just as with Cap and Trade, progressives were the driving force behind the passage of The Patient Protection and Affordable Care Act (In classic progressive use of language, who could disagree with an Act with this name?) The Act was sold on the assertion that it would save the country money and keep insurance costs down. Here are the facts:

"President Obama's national health care law will cost $1.76 trillion over a decade, according to a new projection released today by the Congressional Budget Office, rather than the $940 billion forecast when it was signed into law. ...Today, the CBO released new projections from 2013 extending through 2022, and the results are as critics expected: the ten-year cost of the law's core provisions to expand health insurance

---

[150] American Policy Roundtable. Science and Medicine. By Dr. Chuck McGowen. March 9, 2012.

coverage has now ballooned to $1.76 trillion. That's because we now have estimates for ObamaCare's first nine years of full implementation, rather than the mere six when it was signed into law. Only next year will we get a true ten-year cost estimate, if the law isn't overturned by the Supreme Court or repealed by then. Given that in 2022, the last year available, the gross cost of the coverage expansions are $265 billion, we're likely looking at about $2 trillion over the first decade, or more than double what Obama advertised. (emphasis added)" [151]

The American public was also promised by progressives that their insurance premiums would drop in cost once ObamaCare was passed. Scientific reviews of the data prove that just the opposite occurred:

"Health insurance costs continue to rise as President Obama's healthcare overhaul begins to affect Americans' insurance premiums, according to a study by the Kaiser Family Foundation and the Health Research and Educational Trust (HRET). Leaders in health policy analysis and communication, Kaiser and HRET found that

---

[151] Washington Examiner: By Phillip Klein. March 18, 2010.

annual family insurance premiums have spiked this year at a rate three times higher than in 2010, significantly outpacing wage increases and general inflation." The average annual premiums for employer-sponsored health insurance in 2011 are $5,429 for single coverage and $15,073 for family coverage. Compared to 2010, premiums for single coverage are 8% higher and premiums for family coverage are 9% higher. The 9% growth rate in family premiums for 2011 is significantly higher than the 3% growth rate in 2010. Since 2001, average premiums for family coverage have increased 113%. Average premiums for family coverage are lower for workers in small firms (3–199 workers) than for workers in large firms (200 or more workers) ($14,098 vs. $15,520). Average premiums for high deductible health plans with a savings option (HDHP/Sos) are lower than the overall average for all plan types for both single and family coverage." [152]

The study concluded with this:

---

[152] New American. By Brian Koenig. ObamaCare Causes Health Insurance Premiums to Rise. September 29, 2011.

"The average annual premiums for employer-sponsored health insurance in 2011 are $5,429 for single coverage and $15,073 for family coverage. Compared to 2010, premiums for single coverage are 8% higher and premiums for family coverage are 9% higher. The 9% growth rate in family premiums for 2011 is significantly higher than the 3% growth rate in 2010. Since 2001, average premiums for family coverage have increased 113%. Average premiums for family coverage are lower for workers in small firms (3–199 workers) than for workers in large firms (200 or more workers) ($14,098 vs. $15,520). Average premiums for high deductible health plans with a savings option (HDHP/Sos) are lower than the overall average for all plan types for both single and family coverage." [153]

Progressives have long supported coerced "end of life" measures. Indeed, this derives from their agnostic/atheist dogma and, in large measure, is the direct result of their emptiness and secular humanist attitudes. As with any bureaucracy, costs are monitored and the rationing of health care, is as natural as the DMV rationing notepads or timing

---

[153] Ibid.

employee lunch breaks. It is a fact of life that any group empowered with life and death decision making power will act in the perceived best interest of the group's ethos, not the person being regulated.

In 2009 the issue of end of life policies run by bureaucrats caught the attention of U.S. News and World Report. Reporter Peter Roff wrote this about death panels:

"First, they announced that healthcare reform was necessary in order to control costs that, in the future, would be unsustainable when measured against U.S. GDP.

Second, they failed to take into account the message that the need for cost control would send when measured against the fact that most of America's healthcare dollars are spent providing care to people in the last year to six months of their lives.

Third, House Democrats put into their legislation a section encouraging healthcare providers to engage in end-of-life counseling once every five years, and after significant health events occurred.

It is, admittedly, hard to believe that people would insert language into legislation encouraging the "pull the plug on Grandma" option. It is not hard to believe, however, that a rigid government bureaucracy would develop such a program as part of its implementation of new rules, especially if it were called something else. As healthcare expert and ObamaCare critic Betsy McCaughey wrote Monday for the American Spectator:

> Partisans for the legislation claim that it simply aims to provide Medicare coverage for once-every-five-year conversations with doctors over end-of-life care. Wrong. The new "benefit" is inserted in legislation with the express purpose of controlling healthcare costs (page 1). The bill lists what must be covered in the consultation (pages 425-30). Worse still, the legislation states that the Medicare system will rate your doctor's "quality" and (and adjust reimbursement) based on the percentage of your doctor's patients who create living wills and adhere to them. The President and his supporters claim that the provision is "voluntary." The bill does not have to use the word mandatory to make the counseling mandatory. In fact, the word mandatory is seldom used in any legislation. But if there is a penalty for noncompliance, it is mandatory. In this case the penalty is on your doctor." [154]

---

[154] U.S. News and World Report. Peter Roff. August 19, 2009.

Dr. Nora Janjan, along with Dr. Grace-Marie Turner, have expressed grave concern over the inherent risks to patients created by governmental control over healthcare. Dr. Janjan is a physician and a senior fellow in health care policy at the National Center for Policy Analysis, a free market think tank based in Dallas. Dr. Grace-Marie Turner is president of the Galen Institute, which is funded in part by the pharmaceutical and medical industries. Writing in the Orange County Register, the doctors gave this dire warning:

> "Under ObamaCare, medical care will transition from what is appropriate for the individual patient to what is appropriate from government's perspective. And the cost of care will be a significant factor, with government, not doctors and patients, ultimately deciding if a treatment is worthwhile. The transformation of Medicare from an insurance system to a system directing the practice of medicine is defended as necessary to save the program and to standardize what is "appropriate" care for Medicare patients. But it creates a significant conflict of interest when the government is the payer and also determines what constitutes appropriate care. The autonomy

of patients and clinical judgment of physicians will unquestionably be undermined by the health law. For continued progress in medical innovation and to achieve the personalized care that 21st century medicine will bring, it is vital to move away from centralized government dominance of the health sector and toward a new system that rewards payers and providers for providing quality medical care. That means putting patients, not government, first." [155]

Progressives have insisted that the American public leave their common sense at the door when evaluating any government agency that would regulate health care.

Our common vernacular accepts that any group, but especially governmental groups, agencies and bureaucracies, are fundamentally flawed. Terms like: "Red Tape," "Catch 22" "Technicality" "Snafu" and a host of other like terms, reflect the public's awareness of the maddening decision making process found in overseeing agencies, bureaus and overseers.

Who among us has not experienced the capricious, unfair and outright stupid decisions made by government agencies that regulate our lives? When you receive an "official" notice letter

---

[155] Orange County Register. ObamaCare will usurp control of medicine. Drs. Nora Janjan and Grace-Marie Turner. February 8, 2012.

from a government agency, how does that make you feel? When is the last time you had a positive experience in dealing with a government agency? Now imagine that you have to lobby or persuade some government worker that your doctor's desire to perform this or that procedure is necessary when the government worker decides that she or he knows better. One of the most strident proponents of government run healthcare was the late Senator from Massachusetts, Ted Kennedy. Senator Kennedy died of brain cancer. The Senator was not subjected to end of life counseling, living will assessments nor threatened cutbacks on his physician's fees for the costly care he received the last 6 months of his life. Why? You know the answer to that question. But the question citizens in favor of government run healthcare should really ask themselves is this: What will happen to me if I become seriously ill and I am not a Kennedy? Answer: You and your doctors will be subjected to the capricious judgment of government bureaucrats who will conduct a cost benefit analysis on your life. If you think that won't happen you have proven yourself to be hopelessly infected with the progressive virus.

Progressives are banking on one other benefit from The Patient Protection and Affordable Care Act other than it providing them a means to coerce passive compliance from the public. Ever notice how you behave when you want something from that rude government worker who treats you like you are gum on the bottom of her shoe? You tend to be compliant and supplicant. You smile, tolerate the worker's rude and often times cold and uninformed attitude. That is because when they sit there behind the glass, they have the power. They can give you the permit or they can refuse it. They can purposefully run you through so much red-tape that you will consider just giving up.

Now imagine if you are lobbying to keep your mother alive and the person you are lobbying is a government worker with a fat pension who cannot be fired unless heaven and earth are moved. The bureaucrat is not a doctor and she or he knows you can't sue her, have no redress and she has all the power? This nightmare scenario is facing each and every American because of the progressive virus's success at ram-rodding ObamaCare down the American public's throat.

Health and Human Service emails have come to light that show, beyond a shadow of a doubt, that then Speaker Nancy Pelosi, and Health and Human Services (HHS) head Katherine Sebelius, President Obama and other high ranking officials knew The Patient Protection and Affordable Care Act was fatally flawed.

"We see the Administration's own internal experts repeatedly warning Health and Human

Services Secretary Kathleen Sebelius's political appointees of the likelihood of a bailout. The actuaries explain that the provision of ObamaCare known as the CLASS Act is so poorly designed, it is financially "unsound," "unsustainable," and likely to prove "terminal."

Americans must come to realize that progressives have stolen senior citizen's benefits and redistributed those benefits to the constituents of progressive activists. And who are those constituents? One of the largest groups is comprised of illegal aliens residing in the United States.

Dr. Elizabeth Lee Vliet, M.D., a woman's health care specialist, writing for the Association of Surgeons and Physicians, gave American citizens a wakeup call:

> "What does illegal immigration have to do with your costs and your access to medical care when you need it?
>
> *Estimates are that 20-40% of uncompensated ("free") medical services are provided to people in the US illegally. The actual number may be much higher.* Shockingly, hospitals and clinics don't ask about citizenship...a medical version of "Don't Ask, Don't Tell." In both Tucson and Dallas where I have practiced medicine, hospitals are

struggling under massive costs of uncompensated medical services for uninsured people who, by federal law, cannot be turned away for lack of insurance or ability to pay. How much does this uncompensated care actually cost taxpayers? The incredible answer: no one knows. We only have "estimates" of the costs to taxpayers to treat illegal immigrants because hospitals and public health clinics do not ask for proof of citizenship before providing care.

What are consequences to taxpaying citizens?

1. Increased cost and reduced access to trauma care. Tucson has lost all but one Level I Trauma Center to serve all of southern Arizona, in large part due to massive, unsustainable losses from uncompensated care. Auto accidents involving overloaded vans of illegal aliens happen regularly in southern Arizona. Injured are flown by air ambulance to University Medical Center's Trauma Center and treated with state of the art care....all at taxpayer expense.

2. A registered nurse involved with the Pima County health system since the 1970s who must remain anonymous because of her role, said she

has never seen any staff member at either El Rio Clinic or Pima County Health Department ask for proof of citizenship before providing free medical services (immunizations, Well Baby checks, food stamps, WIC services, birth control, and even elective abortions). Costs are paid by taxpayers. When funds are depleted, low income American citizens have fewer services and longer waits as a result.

3. This same RN also said: "I personally know Mexican men who married 16 year old girls, got them pregnant, brought them to Tucson for the baby to become a US citizen. They live in Mexico but come here for their health care. Taxpayers pay for this medical care many ways, at the Public Health Department, and with school nurses who provide care."

4. Uncompensated medical services for illegal immigrants mean higher premiums for all of us due to cost shifting among all third party payers. To cover the deficits from "free" medical services they provide, the administration at University Physicians Health System Kino campus is

analyzing how much to increase employee health insurance premiums as of July 1.

5. ObamaCare cuts benefits to American citizens: $500 billion in Medicare cuts and slashing the Medicare Advantage program. Medicare Advantage, chosen by one in five seniors, is the most popular plan for low and moderate income seniors, and covers about half of our Hispanic or African-American elderly. My patients on Medicare have worked and paid into the system over their working careers, yet these cuts mean less health-care available to them now. We certainly cannot afford to cover those here illegally.

6. Hospitals in Tucson and Dallas also provide uncompensated ("free") maternity services to pregnant women here illegally. Their babies then become US citizens entitled to all of the services available for low income American families – food stamps, WIC, immunizations, office visits, medications, etc. This drives up costs to all of us: higher premiums for private insurance companies, and higher taxes for government insurance like Arizona's Medicaid (AHCCCS).

7. Professional estimates are that over half of the pregnant women served at Parkland Hospital in Dallas are in this country illegally. With over 16,000 deliveries a year, Parkland is one of the nation's busiest maternity services with prenatal clinics for low income women to receive free prenatal care, nutrition, medication, birthing classes, child care classes, and free supplies (formula, diapers, bottles, car seats). Taxpayers pay the bills. How many of these women are legal citizens and how many are not? No one knows. No one asks about citizenship. It is significant that the 4 states with the highest number of uninsured patients are the southern Border States that also have the highest burden of illegal immigrants: California, Arizona, New Mexico and Texas. The bottom line is that working, taxpaying, legal citizens are bearing the brunt of the failure of our government officials to document citizenship before providing medical services. How long before your medical care is delayed or denied because our health systems have collapsed from deficits due to uncompensated medical care? Arizona's massive deficits, greatly increased by

healthcare services for illegals, is the canary in the mine, warning of a potential explosion that may collapse the system for all. It's straight out of the Cloward-Piven playbook: destroy the system by overwhelming it. Your state – and your healthcare –may be next." [156]

---

[156] Association of American Physicians and Surgeons. By: By Elizabeth Lee Vliet, M.D. June 10, 2010.

CHAPTER NINETEEN

Reflections of Progressivism

WE HAVE DOCUMENTED THAT progressives choose subjects to leverage their quest for power that appear to be in need of a good dose of social justice. Every public school kid has been indoctrinated to believe in a lengthy list of progressive infected causes. To quote Al Gore: "The Earth has a fever." The Cap and Trade boondoggle is supposed to lower that fever. But Cap and Trade, in addition to providing progressives draconian control over much of America, will also provide Al Gore, Nancy Pelosi and their insider progressive comrades a path to unbelievable wealth.

The so-called Affordable Care Act is neither affordable nor does it protect and insure healthcare. We assert that progressives do not care about the environment, the Earth's temperature, your mother's health or you.

Those infected with the progressive virus are revolutionaries who are driven to first foment the revolution then take totalitarian control of America, then the world.

The young and gullible who buy into the progressive's façade do, on the other hand, care about the environment, healthcare affordability, racial fairness, treatment of the poor and they abhor acts of greed. And so should conservatives and anti-progressives.

The fact that progressives have been able to hijack those issues represents a failure on the part of anti-progressives who have permitted themselves to be portrayed as bad people. To be sure, and to quote Dr. Maslow at the end of his life: "[T]here was danger in our thinking and acting as if there were no paranoids or psychopaths or SOBs to mess things up." The SOBs, paranoids and psychopaths among conservatives have proven to be perfect foils for the progressive's psychological strategies. I would add to that list those conservative or apolitical Americans who are simply greedy and lack empathy or compassion. This group of people is remarkably like their progressive brethren when compared on personality tests.

Anti-progressives need to call-out those Americans and their businesses who have proven to be the perfect foils for progressives. Medical insurance companies are notorious for making capricious and stingy decisions when adjudicating their insured's claims. Unlike redress against government regulators, insureds could sue their private insurer if they believed their rights had been violated. Regardless, medical insurance companies have been the perfect foil for those ram-rodding government run health care down the American public's throat. These unattractive people have been used by progressives to persuade the American public to accept their revolution. For conservatives, they represent the enemy within.

When I was a paperboy back in the Midwest, the nicest "customer" I had was a woman who was a devout Christian. She paid me on time, always greeted me with a smile and would occasionally offer me a chocolate chip cookie. I was an animal lover and took note of the fact that she took in strays.

She had this one dog, a mixed breed mutt she found on the streets. When she found him he was emaciated and had a limp. His blond fur was so pale and matted that he looked like an old rug left out in the rain. I had seen him on my paper route and would always try to give him something to eat, but he ran from me. Well, that dog became known as "Mr. Softee." He got that name because every day around 4:00 P.M., when the Mr. Softee truck would come down our street, playing its song ("The creamiest, dreamiest soft ice cream you get from Mr. Softee, for a refreshing delight supreme, look for Mr. Softee), Mrs. Jefferson and "Mr. Softee" would walk to the curb and my customer would buy the pampered pooch his vanilla ice cream cone. If any of the neighborhood kids, some of whom were Black, were hanging around when the Mr. Softee truck pulled over, we all got offered ice cream and more often than not while we were eating the treat we'd feel a soft pat on our heads coming from Mrs. Jefferson. You could just tell Mrs. Jefferson loved all of us kids equally, regardless of race. By the way, did I mention that Mrs. Jefferson was a Black woman?

I compare that experience and how it formed my view of Christians with the feeling I have when I watch most tele-evangelists. [157] I single out tele-evangelists because as a group they have been the perfect foil for agnostic/atheist progressives. It is as though I am watching a never-ending telethon where this iteration of Christianity offers salvation, vials of special oil, prayer cloths and the promise of wealth and health in exchange for $1,000 dollars of seed money. I saw one of these ready-made foils for progressives recently tell a story about how someone who "put a little something" in an envelope for the pastor mysteriously received a new, black-on-black Corvette. You can't make this stuff up.

After careful review I can represent with some surety that the going rate for salvation among tele-evangelists is $1,000 dollars. And it is not just the tele-evangelist's never-ending pitch for money that makes them the perfect foil. Where Mrs. Jefferson was pleasant looking, certainly not threatening, many

---

[157] I would be remiss were I not to **exclude** from my critique "The 700 Club, led by Pat Robertson. His show has proven to be the exception.

tele-evangelists look like they should be working at a carnival, but with one difference, they dress really nice, and I mean *really* nice.

They sport opulent gold rings and cufflinks and wear fine leather shoes. Many of them have had over the top cosmetic surgery, Botox injections, hair-plugs and sport those super-white caps filling every inch of their mouth. Some of the male ministers do something else that seems out of place, to this trained eye they make passes at some of the more attractive choir girls. By the way, many of these ministers strike me as frustrated performers who use their captive audience to sing off-key or prance around the pulpit, that is stage, like a rap-artist.

Then there are the women tele-evangelists. Their hair is often platinum blond, puffed up like a jumbo sized helping of cotton candy. Their dresses are a cross between "Little House on the Prairie" and a Saloon girl's evening gown circa 1898. And that smile, there is something so disconcerting about a cheek-to-cheek smile that only moves when the mouth says "Amen."

My point is that progressives are either agnostic or atheist. Progressives never, ever, pit their lifestyle of self-indulgence, compass-less values, drugs and emptiness sans community organizing up against the lifestyle of Mrs. Jefferson. Instead, progressives use the television ministers as their foil and they do so with great success. But they don't just target tele-evangelists to proselytize atheism and their progressive revolution.

Progressive foils are everywhere and in some places you would not expect. 21st century America ushered in a number of well-known people who were only famous for being famous. Trust fund children who behaved badly in public occupied a disproportionately large bandwidth in the mass media. Paris Hilton, The Kardashians and a host of other wealthy libertines represented the perfect foils for progressives push to confiscate the wealth of successful people. Here is what Senator Lautenberg had to say about one of these libertine foils:

> 'The GOP is holding everyone's tax cut hostage until Paris Hilton gets hers,' Sen. Frank Lautenberg, D-N.J., said after Republicans blocked legislation to extend some expiring tax cuts." [158]

Progressives are masterful at using libertine trust fund children as proof that taxes are too low for the rich. Blame the parents of these miscreants who have proven to be the perfect foils for progressive revolutionaries.

The other evening I saw Alexandra Pelosi (Nancy's daughter) do a hit piece on Christians living in Mississippi. Bill Maher had sent Alexandra down to Mississippi in order to get canon fodder

---

[158] Associated Press. Reporter: David Espo. Failed Tax Cut Vote May Pave Way for Compromise. December 4, 2010.

for his show *Real Time*, airing on HBO. Alexandra found some poor people who were living in squalor who voiced the opinion that the government should stay out of the healthcare business and that if we just left things up to God, things would take care of themselves. Maher's audience guffawed at the Mississippians chosen by Ms. Pelosi. The elite progressives and their sympathizers in his TV audience had their existential emptiness filled for a time by making fun of other people. I would like to see Alexandra Pelosi or Bill Maher interview Mrs. Jefferson, as opposed to the foils they so carefully choose to represent their enemies.

In an interesting twist, shortly after Ms. Pelosi's segment on Mississippians, she did a report on African-American's living in New York City. Many expressed a sense of entitlement to government benefits because of slavery, admitted to having multiple children with multiple "baby mommas," and also declared that they did not intend to work. According to Ms. Pelosi, HBO executives tried to stop the airing of her New York segment. These are the same people who welcomed with open arms her exposé on residents of Mississippi. And speaking of Mississippi.

Maher, Pelosi and their audience don't know a damn thing about Mississippians. White southerners could teach the L.A. crowd a thing or two about hospitality, warmth and sharing.

Many Mississippians are poor, but I thought that made them a part of the 99-percent, and that made them "good." Which brings me to this point.

It is clear that progressives and their sympathizers run Hollywood and the mass media at every level. Anti-progressives can sit back and complain about the propaganda coming from the Westside of Los Angeles and Manhattan all day long, but that will do no good. If anti-progressives won't or can't turn off their televisions, stop going to the movies or stop consuming Hollywood's propaganda, then anti-progressives need to put their money where their mouth is and begin producing media content that is not infected with the progressive virus.

Don't expect to be able to break into the closed shop that is Hollywood, it is not going to happen. But money for anti-progressive projects does exist and creativity is not limited to the Westside of Los Angeles or Midtown Manhattan, no matter what they may want you to believe. If the public is going to consume media no matter what, then offer them entertaining and informative content that is not laced with a dose of progressive poison.

One other thing, speak the truth and stop rolling over. Progressives use psychological techniques that exploit their enemy's weakness. For example, Anglo-Christians *willingly* gave up Christmas on the Prado, a celebration of Christmas that had taken place for decades in San Diego, a relatively conservative California community, with a strong Catholic demographic, especially among Latinos. In its place progressives created "December Nights." By replacing Christmas on the Prado with their secular humanist spectacle, progressives removed one more cultural obstacle to their ultimate desire to turn America into a secular nation, void of all its Christian past. By the way, "Winter or December Nights," as it is now called, is remarkably like Saturnalia, the Pagan festival that celebrated the winter solstice. So much for "thinking forward."

When Southern California's Public Schools in mostly Black districts stopped celebrating Easter with Easter-egg hunts, removed Christmas trees and in their place put up Kwanza decorations, the progressive's had done it again.

> Kwanza was invented in 1966 by a black radical by
> the name of Ron Karenga, aka Dr. Maulana
> Karenga. Karenga was a founder of United Slaves,
> a violent nationalist rival to the Black Panthers.

The name "Kwanza comes from the Swahili phrase "Matunda ya kwanza," which means: "The first fruits of the harvest." Notice that as with "December Nights" and its relationship to Saturnalia, Kwanza reverted back to one of man's earliest secular celebrations, the fall harvest.

Kwanza pillaged over two hundred years of Black Christian's natural heritage in America. I say natural because the last person still living in America who was forcefully removed from Africa and brought to America died sometime around the early 1820s.

Native born Black Americans have a long history in America, many of them living here a century before the great European immigrant influx of the early 20th Century. When Anglo-Americans who were liberal, not progressive, bought hook, line and sinker the progressive's attempt to separate Black people from their American Christian heritage, Anglo liberals rolled over. It was as though Anglos bought the lie that Blacks were NOT truly rooted in Christianity, and were waiting to be reunited with their African roots. As the late Red Fox used to say in his standup routine: "The other day somebody told me to go back where I came from....I told the mother f_ _ _ _r I was from Saint Louis."

Progressives will strip Blacks of their natural Christian heritage just as easily as they will strip Anglo-Christians of their heritage anywhere anytime. Christians are a threat to progressives because they have values and know how to say what all progressives fear: "Don't do that, it is wrong." Ponder these facts:

African-Americans are overwhelmingly Christian.

They are the most religiously devout racial group

in the nation when it comes to attending services, praying and believing that God exists. Compared to the rest of the U.S. population, which is generally considered highly religious, African-Americans engage in religious activities more frequently and express higher levels of religious belief. The Pew Research Center's U.S. Religious Landscape Survey, conducted in 2007 on more than 35,000 people, found that 79 percent of African-Americans say religion is very important in their lives while 56 percent of all U.S. adults said the same. Even among African-Americans who are unaffiliated with any particular faith, 45 percent of them say religion is very important compared to 16 percent of the religiously unaffiliated population overall. Among the various racial and ethnic groups, African-Americans are the most likely to say they belong to a formal religious affiliation. An overwhelming 87 percent of African-Americans identify with a religious group. Following close behind are Latinos, with 85 percent of its population associating with a religion (Catholocism). In comparison, 83 percent of the overall U.S.

population report affiliation with a religion. Nearly six out of ten African-Americans (59 percent) say they belong to a historically black Protestant church, according to the study. The next most popular affiliation is Evangelical Protestant churches (15 percent). Slightly more than one out of ten (12 percent) say they are unaffiliated to a religious group. [159]

Black Christian ministers who actually preside over churches in their community and don't play one on TV overwhelmingly agree with Bill Cosby. They know exactly what is going on. Their Christian/American roots run deep.

So what is a progressive to do with this religious community? Progressives exploit Black youth with destructive, misogynistic messages and encourage them to adopt a lifestyle that rejects their Christian roots. Why would they purposefully do this? Because stripping African-Americans of their Christian roots is necessary in order to foment *progressive's* revolution. Destroy the Black family and you have the perfect canvas upon which you can write the progressive's valueless, self-indulgent, anti Anglo/Black Christian plan. Progressives have and continue to destroy young Black men with an efficiency that would make

---

[159] Pew Research Center's Forum on Religion & Public Life . The U.S. Religious Landscape Survey, conducted in 2007 on more than 35,000 people.

avowed racists salivate. Foment hatred between Anglos and Blacks and voila, you have a ready-made revolution. First, you have to encourage the destruction of the Black family. And to do that, you must undermine African American's Christian roots.

When progressives like Nancy Pelosi overlook, therefore encourage, her constituents to kill themselves with their self-destructive, drug addled and promiscuous behavior, she is sacrificing thousands of young gay men's lives because progressives can't say: "Don't do that, it is wrong." Some things you ought not do because it will kill you and hurt those around you who love you.

When progressives destroy or weaken their victim's ability to discriminate good from bad, friend from foe, when they blatantly wield power using two different standards, one for progressives and another one for everyone else, they leave America vulnerable.

Progressives are weakening America. Just like the bacteriophage virus that hijacks its victims DNA, progressives are making their once in a lifetime big push to change America's DNA. The progressive virus is not bullet proof, however. America can boost its immune system and kill the virus or a natural calamity will do it for America. Natural calamities have a way of stripping away the belief that "I am God".

Progressives have so weakened America's ability to discriminate friend from foe, good from evil, that America's enemies have become emboldened. Our enemies are not plagued with the progressive virus's inability to discriminate good from bad, and to them, Americans are so bad we don't deserve to survive.

Progressives in America invite aggression by their behavior. For example, some feminists in America bristle if they are called "ma'am" as opposed to "Senator." Some feminists scream at the top of their lungs if they are referred to as "lady." But on the other hand, these same feminist progressives (I have in mind numerous progressive media types and politicians) have no problem donning Islamic cloaking when around Muslim men. These are the same Muslim men who won't let "their" women drive, stone them to death for adultery, are allowed to beat women and will kill their daughter in a so-called "honor killing" if she dares to date outside her religion. Sound crazy?

Mental disorders, not orthopedic, neurological disorders or heart disease and cancer, are the leading cause of disability in the U.S. and Canada. [160] An estimated 26.2 percent of Americans ages 18 and older — about one in four adults — suffer from a

---

[160] The World Health Organization. The global burden of disease: 2004 update, Table A2: Burden of disease in DALYs by cause, sex and income group in WHO regions, estimates for 2004. Geneva, Switzerland: WHO, 2008. http://www.who.int/healthinfo/global_burden_disease/GBD_report_2004update_AnnexA.pdf.

diagnosable mental disorder in a given year.[161] When applied to the 2004 U.S. Census residential population estimate for ages 18 and older, this figure translates to 57.7 million people.[162] Many people suffer from more than one mental disorder at a given time. Nearly half (45 percent) of those with any mental disorder meet criteria for 2 or more disorders, with severity strongly related to comorbidity.[163]

The emptiness created by the progressive virus, the same emptiness experienced by Bill Clinton, paired with progressive's "do your own thing" mandate, manifests in hospital emergency rooms every day in America:

> "In 2009, there were nearly 4.6 million drug-related ED visits nationwide. These visits included reports of drug abuse, adverse reactions to drugs, or other drug-related consequences. Almost 50 percent were attributed to adverse reactions to

---

[161] Kessler RC, Chiu WT, Demler O, Walters EE. Prevalence, severity, and comorbidity of twelve-month DSM-IV disorders in the National Comorbidity Survey Replication (NCS-R). Archives of General Psychiatry, 2005 Jun;62(6):617-27.

[162] U.S. Census Bureau Population Estimates by Demographic Characteristics. Table 2: Annual Estimates of the Population by Selected Age Groups and Sex for the United States: April 1, 2000 to July 1, 2004 (NC-EST2004-02) Source: Population Division, U.S. Census Bureau Release Date: June 9, 2005. http://www.census.gov/popest/national/asrh/

[163] Kessler RC, Chiu WT, Demler O, Walters EE. Prevalence, severity, and comorbidity of twelve-month DSM-IV disorders in the National Comorbidity Survey Replication (NCS-R). Archives of General Psychiatry, 2005 Jun;62(6):617-27.

pharmaceuticals taken as prescribed, and 45 percent involved drug abuse. DAWN estimates that of the 2.1 million drug abuse visits—

27.1 percent involved nonmedical use of pharmaceuticals (i.e., prescription or OTC medications, dietary supplements)

21.2 percent involved illicit drugs

14.3 percent involved alcohol, in combination with other drugs.

ED visits involving nonmedical use of pharmaceuticals (either alone or in combination with another drug) increased 98.4 percent between 2004 and 2009, from 627,291 visits to 1,244,679, respectively. ED visits involving adverse reactions to pharmaceuticals increased 82.9 percent between 2005 and 2009, from 1,250,377 to 2,287,273 visits, respectively.

The majority of drug-related ED visits were made by patients 21 or older (80.9 percent, or 3,717,030 visits). Of these, slightly less than half involved drug abuse. Patients aged 20 or younger accounted for 19.1 percent (877,802 visits) of all drug-related visits in 2009; about half of these visits involved drug abuse."[164]

These data are the tip of the iceberg when it comes to how the progressive virus has compromised America's immune system.

Those who were in New York City on September 11, 2001 will attest to the closeness they felt with other Americans on that day. Racial and class division, those differences so efficiently created, then exploited by progressives, melted for a time. If your face was covered with that fine gray dust and you were running, you were an American brother or sister. America reached into its cultural roots to find strength that fall day, because that is where its strength resides. Progressives slithered away immediately post 9/11. Such disasters are a very costly way to get rid of the progressive virus infecting America.

Americans can choose to boost their immune system by returning to their roots. There is objective good and bad. Pink lungs are good and brown lungs are bad. Respecting yourself and others is the way Mrs. Jefferson lived her life. She led through example. Who would you trust to watch your teenage daughter if you had to choose between Mrs. Jefferson or (name your progressive activist)? Discipline and respect for learning will do more than all the money in the world paid to teacher's

---

[164] National Institute on Drug Abuse. *Drug Related Hospital Emergency Room Visits*. May, 2011.

unions. Discipline and respect comes from mothers and fathers. Vouchers and school choice are the immediate antidote to public school indoctrination and progressive brainwashing. In the longer term, replacing aging Weathermen with the Mrs. Jeffersons of the world will do more for education reform than anything else. Show me a high-performing school and I will show you a charter or parochial school run by an anti-progressive.

Groups are dangerous, no matter how well intentioned or how non-threatening their name. Government agencies and bureaucracies are most dangerous because they are groups with plenary power. The fact that progressives tout government as citizen's savior is like touting cyanide as a pain reliever.

The late Adlai Stevenson said this about communism, the end phase of a successful progressive revolution.

> "Communism is the death of the soul. It is the organization of total conformity – in short, of tyranny – and it is committed to making tyranny universal."

I leave you with these words spoken to the citizens of Cuba by the Pope on March 28, 2012. I encourage the reader to appreciate the meaning these words have given that they were spoken in a Marxist/Communist country:

"The truth is a desire of the human person, the search for which always supposes the exercise of authentic freedom. Many, however, prefer shortcuts, trying to avoid this task. Some, like Pontius Pilate, ironically question the possibility of even knowing what truth is (cf. Jn 18:38), proclaiming that man is incapable of knowing it or denying that there exists a truth valid for all. This attitude, as in the case of skepticism and relativism, changes hearts, making them cold, wavering, distant from others and closed. They, like the Roman governor, wash their hands and let the water of history drain away without taking a stand.

On the other hand, there are those who wrongly interpret this search for the truth, leading them to irrationality and fanaticism; they close themselves up in "their truth", and try to impose it on others. These are like the blind scribes who, upon seeing Jesus beaten and bloody, cry out furiously, "Crucify him!" (cf. Jn 19:6).

Anyone who acts irrationally cannot become a disciple of Jesus. Faith and reason are necessary and complementary in the pursuit of truth. God created man with an innate vocation to the truth and he gave him reason for this purpose. Certainly, it is not irrationality but rather the yearning for truth which the Christian faith promotes. Each human being has to seek the truth and to choose it when he or she finds it, even at the risk of embracing sacrifices.

Furthermore, the truth which stands above humanity is an unavoidable condition for attaining freedom, since in it we discover the foundation of an ethics on which all can converge and which contains clear and precise indications concerning life and death, duties and rights, marriage, family and society, in short, regarding the inviolable dignity of the human person. This ethical patrimony can bring together different cultures, peoples and religions, authorities and citizens, citizens among themselves, and believers in Christ and non-believers." [165]

THE END

---

[165] National Catholic Register. Papal Visit to Cuba. Papal Homily Excerpt. March 28, 2012.

INDEX

D

CPSIA information can be obtained at www.ICGtesting.com
Printed in the USA
BVOW06s0048160416

444378BV00012B/235/P